W9-AAX-929

IRISH TERRIER

BACK
Strong and level

HINDQUARTERS
Strong and muscular

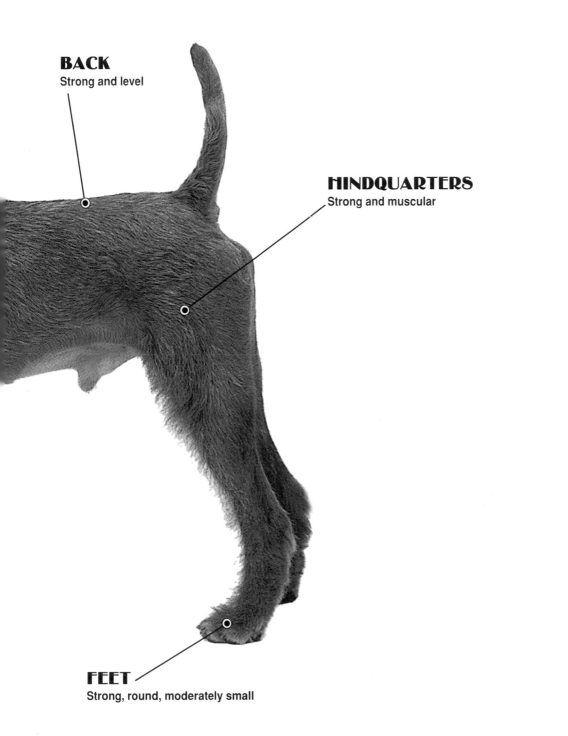

FEET
Strong, round, moderately small

Photographers: Ashby Photography, Booth Photography, Close Encounters of the Furry Kind, Isabelle Francais, Robert and Gloria Geddes, Paul and Peggy Gill, Chris Halvorson, Bruce and Nancy Petersen, Stephen Skolnik, and Karen Taylor

© **T.F.H. Publications, Inc.**

Distributed in the UNITED STATES to the Pet Trade by T.F.H. Publications, Inc., One T.F.H. Plaza, Neptune City, NJ 07753; on the Internet at www.tfh.com; in CANADA Rolf C. Hagen Inc., 3225 Sartelon St. Laurent-Montreal Quebec H4R 1E8; Pet Trade by H & L Pet Supplies Inc., 27 Kingston Crescent, Kitchener, Ontario N2B 2T6; in ENGLAND by T.F.H. Publications, PO Box 74, Havant PO9 5TT; in AUSTRALIA AND THE SOUTH PACIFIC by T.F.H. (Australia), Pty. Ltd., Box 149, Brookvale 2100 N.S.W., Australia; in NEW ZEALAND by Brooklands Aquarium Ltd. 5 McGiven Drive, New Plymouth, RD1 New Zealand; in SOUTH AFRICA, Rolf C. Hagen S.A. (PTY.) LTD. P.O. Box 201199, Durban North 4016, South Africa; in Japan by T.F.H. Publications, Japan—Jiro Tsuda, 10-12-3 Ohjidai, Sakura, Chiba 285, Japan. Published by T.F.H. Publications, Inc.
Manufactured in the
United States of America
by T.F.H. Publications, Inc.

IRISH TERRIER

A COMPLETE AND RELIABLE HANDBOOK

Muriel P. Lee

RX-128

CONTENTS

INTRODUCTION

The Irish! Lively, spirited, boisterous; rambunctious, strong willed and intelligent; ready for a challenge and a devoted family member—this description applies to the Irishman as well as to his dog, the wonderful Irish Terrier, also called the "Daredevil." In 1936, Will Judy wrote, "The Irish Terrier! He is a bundle of pluck and devil-may-care. He is as gay and lively as any other native of the Emerald Isle!"

This book will give you an overview of the breed, its history, description, and the standard. You will also learn about puppy care, training, and how to maintain the health of the breed. With the wonderful color photographs you will see that this red terrier is as handsome as they come and that the puppies are as charming as any of the Irish.

Because of his very active ways, this may not be the dog for everyone. However, if you find that you like a plucky and a smart dog, one that will stand his ground against another animals and that will also be a faithful family member, this just may be the breed for you. And, as true with most other breeds, once you give your heart and home to an Irish Terrier, you will remain devoted to the breed for a lifetime.

Commonly known as the "Daredevil," the Irish Terrier is intelligent, spunky, determined, and extremely devoted. These lively dogs can add a lot of fun and charm to any household.

HISTORY OF THE IRISH TERRIER

In the history of the dog world, the Irish Terrier is not an ancient breed; however, its official beginnings, which trace back to the 1800s, place it among one of the older breeds recognized by the American Kennel Club.

The Irish Terrier is one of several breeds of dogs that are indigenous to Ireland and that are recognized by the American Kennel Club. These breeds fall into three groups: Sporting, which includes the Irish Water Spaniel and the Irish Setter; Hound, which includes the Irish Wolfhound; and Terrier, which includes the Kerry Blue, the Soft Coated Wheaten, and the Irish Terrier.

The Irish Terrier belongs to the group of dogs described as terriers, from the Latin word *terra*, meaning earth. The terrier is a dog that has been bred to work beneath the ground to drive out small and large vermin, rodents, and other animals that can be a nuisance to country living.

All of the dogs in the terrier group, with the exception of the Miniature Schnauzer, originated in the British Isles. Many of the terrier breeds were derived from a similar ancestor and as recently as the mid-1800s, the terriers fell roughly into two basic categories: the rough-coated, short-legged dogs, and the smooth-coated, longer-legged dogs.

The terriers, although they may differ in type, all have the same character. They are bred as game dogs who go after vermin, and who also make good companions for their masters. As early as 1735, the *Sportsman's Dictionary* described the terrier as "a kind of hound, used only or chiefly for hunting the fox or badger. He creeps into the ground and then nips and bites the fox and badger, either by tearing them in pieces with his teeth, or else hauling them and

Opposite: Irish Terriers were originally bred as game dogs to hunt vermin. They also made excellent and loyal companions for their masters. "Amber," Ch. Cocksure's Mystic Diamond walks confidently across the snowy terrain.

pulling them by force out of their lurking holes."

Although the terrier's background may be a bit obscure, most people are certain that in the 1700s and early 1800s there was no definite breed of terrier, but that dogs were bred to go to ground with courage and conviction. Those who were unable to do the job were destroyed and those who could do the proper work were bred to one another with little regard for type. "Unless they were fit and game for the purpose, their heads were not kept long out of the huge butt of water in the stable yard."

As with most of the terrier breeds, the origins of the Irish Terrier are not clear. The Irish have always been bred for sport and have been, and still are, fearless workers against vermin. Clifford Hubbard, the famous "Doggy Bookman" of England, claims the Irish's origins go back to the Irish Madadh, a breed found in ancient Ireland. A. Croxton Smith writes that the Irish was a compromise between the Fox Terrier and the Airedale but built along racier lines than either breed. Still, others assert that his roots come from the old rough-coated or wire-haired Black and Tan Terrier of English origin. Some have even suggested that he had a kinship to the giant Irish Wolfhound, which he resembled in outline, coat, and color. William Haynes wrote in 1925 that the breed hailed from the North of Ireland, because the terriers of Southern Ireland were silvery-smut in color with a smooth coat. They were built upon more cobby lines than the terriers of Northern Ireland, which were reddish in color with a wire coat and a racy outline. With no doubt in his mind, Mr. Haynes stated, "This was the progenitor of the modern Irish Terrier." John Marvin, another well-known terrier man and author of more recent years, thought that the basic blood of the Irish goes back to the Old Scotch Terrier. Whatever his specific heritage may have been, the Irish Terrier came into his own in Ireland around 1870.

In 1873, the first classes for the breed were offered at a dog show in Dublin and confusion reigned. Classes were offered by size, either over or under nine pounds. Colors ranged from red, wheaten, and black and tan to blue brindle, in addition to hard-coated and soft-coated exhibits. The judge surely had his work cut out for him!

In 1878, the noted authority Stonehenge, in his *Dog of the British Islands* printed a description of the Irish Terrier that had been written by R. J. Ridgeway. This description was accepted and approved by 25 Irish Terrier breeders and exhibitors, which included many who became very well known in the breed: Ridgeway, who became known as the "father of the breed," William (Billy) Graham, George Jamison, Dr. R. B. Carey, all of Ireland; and George Krehl and Albert Krehl of England. By 1899, a specialty club was formed in Dublin called The Irish Terrier Club and later in 1899, English fans of the breed organized to support this group.

A good representative for the breed, Ch. Straight Tip stands proudly in an exhibition held at Madison Square Garden in New York City.

An early point of dissension in the breed, along with the weight and size of the dog, was the cropping of ears. By 1888, the Irish Terrier Club had passed a resolution that cropped ears would no longer be acceptable. In 1899, The Kennel Club (England) ruled that any Irish Terrier whelped after December 31, 1899, that had cropped ears would be ineligible to compete in a show. By 1890, large classes of Irish were common at all shows. The weight had been raised to 25 pounds and the bright red coat color was preferable, with the red-wheaten and yellow red being acceptable. At the present time the standard states: "The most desirable weight in show condition is 27 pounds for the dog and 25 pounds for the bitch. Colors should be whole-colored: bright red, golden red, red-wheaten or wheaten."

William Haynes wrote about the early shows: "When he made his debut, the Daredevils were a scratch pack. There was a considerable difference in size, ranging from 18 to 30 pounds. The color might run all the way from light fawn to deep red—not to mention smutty ones and some with various unorthodox markings of white or black. The coat was in some cases like wire and in others short and smooth. Usually the ears were cropped, though they were sometimes left natural. But the Irish type was there and the red-colored, wire-coated dogs were in the popular majority."

The early winners and influential sires and dams carried wonderful and colorful names: Slasher, Killinney Boy, Stinger, Sport, and Spuds. George Jamison's Sport was the dog that caught the eye of the serious fanciers and it is said that Sport set the type for the Irish Terrier, and that type has prevailed to the present time. He had natural ears that were held correctly, he was overall red in color, and he was a "handy" size with good length of leg.

Although the Irish Terrier's origins are not clear, they have been bred in Ireland throughout the ages to hunt vermin.

ME bROthER Pat!

Killiney Boy, considered by some as the father of the breed, was bred to the red bitch Ch. Erin, owned by Billy Graham, and produced a famous litter of six: Playboy, Pretty Lass, Poppy, Gerald, Pagan II, and Peggy. They all won in the ring, but Playboy and Poppy were the best in type and carried the desirable red color, which came to be accepted as the proper color for the breed. Billy Graham, through his successes and travels, is credited with doing more for establishing the modern Irish Terrier than anyone. He thought his Ch. Erin was the best bitch that he had ever seen and bought her straight out of a hamper at a show in Dublin. Erin is considered the mother of the modern breed. Over 90 percent of the breed trace their ancestry back to Killiney Boy and Erin (providing you could find a pedigree page large enough to get all of the names in place).

In 1896, a group of American fanciers met in Boston and organized the Irish Terrier Club of America (ITCA), which was recognized by the American Kennel Club in 1897. The ITCA is one of the older breed clubs recognized by the American Kennel Club and held its centenary celebration in 1997.

Aileen was the first Irish Terrier registered in the United States. The first Irish exhibited in the US was an import named Kathleen, shown in 1884, and the first US champion was an English import named Breda Tiny. James Watson in *The Dog Book*, 1905, gives a very concise history of the breed and the dogs in America prior to 1905.

William Haynes wrote, "In 1895, Mr. O. W. Donner sprang his Milton Droleen, the first American-bred flyer. And a flyer she was! She cleaned the boards here and then invaded England where the old timers hailed her as 'The American Erin,' who she strongly

The Irish Terrier Club of America (ITCA) was organized in 1896 and recognized by the American Kennel Club in 1897. Ch. Culbahn Chancellor.

suggested in looks."

In New York, in 1900, the American-bred Ch. Masterpiece went undefeated for three years, until beaten in 1903 by Rev. Father O'Gorman's dog, Ch. Celtic Badger. Again, Mr. Haynes colorfully writes, "Will I not be pardoned if I digress a moment to say a word about his owner, the good Father O'Gorman. He was one of the best true fanciers, a thorough man, a good fellow in the best sense of the word."

As in all breeds that succeeded in the early part of the 20th century, it took a group of dedicated breeders, those with patience and money, to promote the breed and to import the best dogs from the British Isles. The Irish Terrier has been fortunate to have a group of individuals who worked tirelessly to see that the breed remained true to type and healthy.

Although the number that has contributed to the breed is substantial, only a few will be mentioned in this short history.

Marcus Bruckheimer attended the first Irish Terrier meeting in New York in 1897 and remained active in the breed for over 40 years. Jeremiah O'Callaghan immigrated to the US from County Cork as a child, bred his first litter in 1902, and carried on his breeding program under the Kilvara name for nearly 70 years

The Kilvara bloodline has been very influential in the breed. Kilvara Magic Master captures the graceful stance and strength of an Irish Terrier.

until his death. The Kilvara bloodlines have been very influential in the breed, and for many years the breed winners at Westminter Kennel Club and the Irish Terrier Club of America specialty were from his line. George Kidd wrote that the reason "the Kilvara bloodlines became so influential was that Mr. O'Callahan seemed to have an instinct for mating the right dogs, and, in addition, he outlived his early competitors, while the new, dedicated breeders founded their kennels on the Kilvara dogs." In 1962, he was voted for an Honorary Life Membership into the ITCA and continued to judge until his later years.

The Irish Terrier has benefited from the dedicated breeders who have helped retain the dog's original type throughout the years.

There are many other breeders who made their mark in the breed in the first half of the 20th century. John Best of Milwaukee, founder of the Badger Kennel Club in 1939, bought his first Irish in 1931. Under the Blackacre prefix, John finished 24 champions, of which 19 carried the Blackacre's prefix. Mr. Best had a large terrier library and was considered a leading authority on terrier literature. He was an active member of the ITCA, serving in many capacities on the board.

In more recent years, the breeders of note have been many. Bobby Clyde of New York began breeding the Irish in 1959. A well-known and popular handler, Mr. Clyde continues to remain active in the breed, sharing his expertise on breeding, grooming, and showing. Phyllis Kendrick, Greencastle Kennels, started her breeding program in 1975 and has bred over 30 champions, with her Ch. Riley's Tara of Glenworth producing 10 champions.

Ellis West of Gloccomara Kennels in Wichita, Kansas, bred Ch. Gloccomara Centrifugal Mama, who was owner-handled to Best of Breed at the ITCA specialty. Her daughter, Gloccomara B-Movie Baby, produced 15 champion offspring, a major accomplishment in any breed. His kennel has produced numerous champions and ITCA Best of Breed winners.

Marion Cruse and her daughter formed the Rockledge Kennels in 1959. Their Ch. Rockledge's Mr. Morgan, multiple Best in Show winner, was the sire of 21 champions. His son, Ch. Rockledge's Mick Michael, won 13 Best in Show awards and is the breed's top producing sire, with over 35 champion offspring. Several other Rockledge dogs have been all-breed Best in Show winners, a wonderful record for a kennel!

Attend any of the dog shows where the Irish Terrier has a respectable entry and watch the judging with your catalog. You will quickly see that at the present time there are many active breeders producing fine

It's not difficult to see why Ahtram Moon Prince was a champion Irish Terrier.

specimens who are consistently winning some of the top spots at the shows. The Irish Terrier is still a very healthy breed that is continuously supported by a group of dedicated individuals.

A POSTCRIPT

The Irish Terrier Club of America is the "keeper" of the breed. If you are interested in purchasing an Irish Terrier, you should contact the Secretary of the ITCA and they will give you the name of a reputable breeder in your area that you can contact.

Remember, this is not a popular breed, puppies are not whelped as often as Poodle puppies, and you may have to wait up to six months or more to get the puppy you want. The American Kennel Club in New York can give you the name and address of the current secretary.

If you are interested in more in-depth history, definition of the standard, or grooming assistance, the Irish Terrier Club of America published an excellent book on the breed in 1996, their centenary year. This can be purchased from the ITCA as long as copies are available.

Ch. Wahoo Satellite was a dominant show dog in the 1950s. Owners, Mr. and Mrs. Watson.

CHARACTERISTICS OF THE IRISH TERRIER

I wrote a book on the Boston Terrier and was impressed with the list of words describing the breed. Now, I find an even longer list to describe the Irish Terrier!

The Irish Terrier is a family dog, a guard dog, and a hunter; he is tender, forbearing, spirited, fearless and reckless; he is devoted, gallant and gentle; he is as courageous as a lion and a fighting Irishman to the core; and best of all, he is an incomparable pal! And all of this is contained in a relatively small package!

When dealing with a breed that possesses all of the above characteristics, one can see why the Irish Terrier can be a challenge to its owner and why this may not be the dog for everyone. Some individuals prefer to come home to a lay-about dog that only

This beautiful pair of Irish Terriers uses their hunting instincts to sniff out something interesting. The breed's trainability and fearless character make them considerable hunting partners.

Although this guy looks relaxed hanging out at the beach, Irish Terriers are very energetic dogs. They perform with great enthusiasm, demonstrate courage, and present a rewarding challenge to their owners.

wants to please his master and makes few demands upon him. If this is your preference, the Irish Terrier is not for you. However, if you like a dog that will bring a challenge to your life, and one who will keep you on your toes, read on!

Orignally, the Irish Terrier, as with all terriers, was bred to be a sporting dog—a "vermin exterminator"— a dog to chase and to kill the farm pests that were a problem both to the farmer and the farm animals. A common characteristic for all terriers is their desire to work with great enthusiasm, speed, and courage. They all have large and powerful teeth for the size of their bodies. They have keen hearing and excellent eyesight, and they have stamina and staying power due to their deep chest. No matter how many generations they have been pets, the purpose for which the breed was bred will remain with the dog. I grew up with a Wirehaired Fox Terrier and owned and bred Scottish Terriers for many years and have firsthand knowledge as to how fast a terrier could find and kill a rabbit in the field or chase a squirrel up a tree in the yard. I presently live with two French Bulldogs, dogs bred to be companions and not much else, and neither Frenchie cares how many squirrels live in their garden or if a frog or two hops over their feet while they lie in the sun.

Some individuals have used the Irish for hunting. Mr. Krehl, the famed terrier breeder, wrote about the Irish, "The dog entered the thickets like a spaniel, retrieved like a Labrador and covered terrain like a pointer or setter. Plus, he had courage, was trainable and fearless and was fitted with a wonderful character."

As a household pet, the Irish makes an excellent family member because he is a one-family dog rather than a one-man dog. He is devoted to his family, very alert, and makes a good watchdog. He is faithful and honest and will do everything in his power to protect his family. He is obedient and relatively easy to train. He has a good sense of humor ("full of the Blarney," as some say, like his fellow countrymen), and he likes to be a tease. In addition, he is a true gentleman.

He is probably the only terrier that worked in both World War I and World War II. The 1935 AKC book, *Terriers*, quoted a Col. Richardson: "It must be admitted, that many of our best War-Dogs were Irish Terriers. These little fellows were remarkably easily taught, and were tremendously keen on their work." George Kidd wrote, "Keeper Hammond, with two dogs, Paddy and Nansen, were assigned to the Passchendaele sector on the front line in Belgium in October, 1917. Nansen was killed on the first run. Paddy carried on and never made a mistake in the six months they were in the sector. On one occasion Paddy carried a message to a unit five miles distant in less than thirty minutes, the route including three miles over duckboards."

To sum up the character of the Irish, Robert Leighton said it best: "He is above all things a dog for man's companionship, equally suitable for town and country life, he has a hardy constitution, requires no pampering, and if taught to be obedient and gentlemanly, there is no better housedog. He is naturally intelligent and easily trained, an ideal companion for children. His boisterous spirits lead him sometimes to trail his coat and he is never found wanting when challenged. A demon for sport, as capable on land as in water, he will tackle anything with four legs and a furry skin. Rats are his mortal enemies."

Opposite: A beautiful shiny coat, bright eyes, a clean nose, and a good physique are all descriptions of what a healthy Irish Terrier should look like.

THE STANDARD FOR THE IRISH TERRIER

Each breed approved by the American Kennel Club has a standard that gives the reader a mental picture of what the specific breed should look like. All reputable breeders strive to produce animals that will meet the requirements of the standard. Many breeds were developed for a specific purpose, i.e., hunting, retrieving, going to ground, coursing, guarding, herding, or working. The terriers were all bred to go to ground and to pursue vermin.

In addition to having dogs that look like a proper Irish Terrier, the standard ensures that the Irish will have the personality, disposition, and intelligence that is sought in the breed. As time progressed and breeders became more aware that certain areas of the dog needed a better description or more definition, breeders would meet together and work out a new standard. However, standards for any breed are never changed on a whim and serious study and exchange between breeders takes place before any move is made.

Opposite: To do well in conformation, a dog must adhere to the standard. The Irish Terrier's head is long, but in good proportion to the rest of the body. The jaw must be strong and muscular but not too full.

OFFICIAL STANDARD FOR THE IRISH TERRIER

Head—Long, but in nice proportion to the rest of the body; the skull flat, rather narrow between the ears, and narrowing slightly toward the eyes; free from wrinkle, with the stop hardly noticeable except in profile. The jaws must be strong and muscular, but not too full in the cheek, and of good punishing length. The foreface must not fall away appreciably between or below the eyes; instead, the modeling should be delicate. An exaggerated foreface, or a noticeably short foreface, disturbs the proper balance of the head and is not desirable. The foreface and the skull from occiput to stop should be approximately equal in

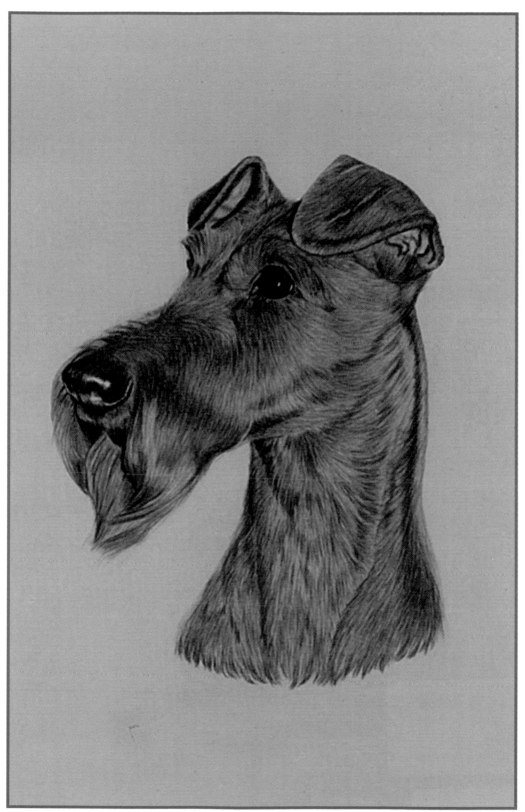

length. Excessive muscular development of the cheeks, or bony development of the temples, conditions which are described by the fancier as "cheeky," or "strong in head," or "thick in skull" are objectionable. The "bumpy" head, in which the skull presents two lumps of bony structure above the eyes, is to be faulted. The hair on the upper and lower jaws should be similar in quality and texture to that on the body, and of sufficient length to present an appearance of additional strength and finish to the foreface. Either the profuse goat-like beard, or the absence of beard, is unsightly and undesirable.

Teeth—Should be strong and even, white and sound; and neither overshot nor undershot.

Lips—Should be close and well-fitting, almost black in color.

Nose—Must be black.

Eyes—Dark brown in color; small, not prominent; full of life, fire and intelligence, showing an intense expression. The light or yellow eye is most objectionable, and is a bad fault.

Ears—Small and V-shaped; of moderate thickness; set well on the head, and dropping forward closely toward the outside corner of the eye. The top of the folded ear should be well above the level of the skull. A "dead" ear, hound-like in appearance, must be severely penalized. It is not characteristic of the Irish Terrier. The hair should be much shorter and somewhat darker in color than that on the body.

Neck—Should be of fair length and gradually widening toward the shoulders; well and proudly carried, and free from throatiness. Generally there is a slight frill in the hair at each side of the neck, extending almost to the corner of the ear.

Shoulders and Chest—Shoulders must be fine, long, and sloping well into the back. The chest should be deep and muscular, but neither full nor wide.

Body—The body should be moderately long. The short back is not characteristic of the Irish Terrier and is extremely objectionable. The back must be strong and straight, and free from an appearance of slackness or "dip" behind the shoulders. The loin should be strong and muscular, and slightly arched, the ribs fairly sprung, deep rather than round, reaching to the level of the elbows. The bitch may be slightly longer than the dog.

Hindquarters—Should be strong and muscular; thighs powerful; hocks near the ground; stifles mod-

Ch. Scolaidhe's Fighting O'Flynn demonstrates perfect form. The body should be fairly long and the back strong and straight. Owner, Stephen Skolnik.

erately bent.

Stern—Should be docked, taking off about one quarter. It should be set on rather high, but not curled. It should be of good strength and substance; of fair length and well covered with harsh, rough hair.

Feet and Legs—The feet should be strong, tolerably round, and moderately small; toes arches and turned neither out nor in, with dark toenails. The pads should be deep, and must be perfectly sound and free from corns. Cracks alone do not necessarily indicate unsound feet. In fact, all breeds have cracked pads occasionally, from various causes.

Legs moderately long, well set from the shoulders, perfectly straight, with plenty of bone and muscle; the elbows working clear of the sides; pasterns short, straight, and hardly noticeable. Both fore and hind legs should move straight forward when traveling; the stifles should not turn outward. "Cowhocks"—that is, the hocks turned in and the feet turned out—are intolerable. The legs should be free from feather and covered with hair of similar texture to that on the body to give proper finish to the dog.

Coat—Should be dense and wiry in texture, rich in quality, having a broken appearance, but still lying fairly close to the body, the hairs growing so closely and strongly together that when parted with the fingers the skin is hardly visible; free of softness or silkiness, and not so long as to alter the outline of the body, particularly in the hindquarters. On the sides of the body the coat is never as harsh as on the back and quarters, but it should be plentiful and of good texture. At the base of the stiff outer coat there should be a growth of finer and softer hair, lighter in color, termed the undercoat. Single coats, which are without any undercoat, and wavy coats are undesirable; the curly and the kinky coats are most objectionable.

Color—Should be whole-colored: bright red, golden red, red wheaten, or wheaten. A small patch of white on the chest, frequently encountered in all whole-colored breeds, is permissible but not desirable. White on any other part of the body is most objectionable. Puppies sometimes have black hair at birth, which should disappear before they are full grown.

Size—The most desirable weight in show condition is 27 pounds for the dog and 25 pounds for the bitch. The height at the shoulder should be approximately 18 inches. These figures serve as a guide to both breeder and judge. In the show ring, however, the informed judge readily identifies the oversized or undersized Irish Terrier by its conformation and general appearance. Weight is not the last word in judgment. It is of the greatest importance to select, insofar as possible, terriers of moderate and generally accepted size, possessing the other various characteristics.

The color of an Irish Terrier's coat ranges from bright red, golden red, red wheaten, or wheaten. Ch. Gloclomora Stardust Express owned by Nancy and Bruce Petersen shows off her vibrant coat.

General Appearance—The over-all appearance of the Irish Terrier is important. In conformation he must be more than a sum of his parts. He must be all-of-a-piece, a balanced vital picture of symmetry, proportion and harmony. Furthermore, he must convey character. This terrier must be active, lithe and wiry in movement, with great animation; sturdy and strong in substance and bone structure, but at the same time free from clumsiness, for speed, power and endurance are most essential. The Irish Terrier must be neither "cobby" nor "cloddy," but should be built on lines of speed with a graceful, racing outline.

Temperament—The temperament of the Irish Terrier reflects his early background: he was family pet, guard dog, and hunter. He is good tempered, spirited and game. It is of the utmost importance that the Irish Terrier show fire and animation. There is a heedless, reckless pluck about the Irish Terrier which is characteristic, and which, coupled with the headlong dash, blind to all consequences, with which he rushes at his adversary, has earned for the breed the proud epithet of "Daredevil." He is of good temper, most affectionate, and absolutely loyal to mankind. Tender and forebearing with those he loves, this rugged, stout-hearted terrier will guard his master, his mistress and children with utter contempt for danger or hurt. His life is one continuous and eager offering of loyal and faithful companionship and devotion. He is ever on guard, and stands between his home and all that threatens.

The Irish Terrier's lively spirit keeps them young at heart. Seven-and-a-half-year-old Ch. Katie Corleen of Gillmere takes the prize at the Montgomery County Kennel Club in 1989.

Approved December 10, 1968

FIRST VETERAN

MONTGOMERY COUNTY
KENNEL CLUB
OCTOBER
1989
DAVE ASHBEY

CARE
OF THE
IRISH TERRIER

By and large, the Irish Terrier is considered to be a healthy breed, relatively free from genetic problems and often known for longevity. William Haynes wrote in 1925, "The terrier owner is a 'lucky Devil' for his dogs do not, as a rule, spend a great deal of time in the hospital. All members of the terrier family, from the giant of the race, the Airedale, way down to little Scottie, owe a big debt to Nature for having blessed them with remarkably robust constitutions. Even when really sick, they make wonderfully rapid recoveries. It is almost a joke to keep such a naturally healthy dog as a terrier in the pink of condition. All he needs is dry, clean kennels with decent bedding, good, nourishing food at regular hours, all the fresh water he wants to drink, plenty of exercise, and a little grooming. Given these few things and a terrier will be disgustingly well, full of high spirits, and happy as a clam at high tide."

The Irish Terrier is a thrifty dog. Give him care, use your common sense, and have a good, reliable veterinarian available. Take your dog in when you think that you have a problem, follow instructions, and recovery will usually be very rapid.

If your veterinarian is not available at odd hours for emergencies, know where the emergency veterinarian is located and keep his telephone number handy. Many veterinarians in large cities no longer have an emergency service and you must rely on these special facilities for late evening, weekend, and holiday services. Keep your dog groomed and clean. Keep him out of the sun in the summer and certainly never leave him in the car during a hot day.

Your dog should be kept in either a fenced-in yard or on a leash. It's foolish and often against the law to let a dog run loose. You take the chance of him becoming lost or run over by a car. Too often the story

Opposite: Before you purchase your Irish Terrier, you must make a commitment to care for him properly.

is heard about the dog that lives at the end of the cul-de-sac where only one delivery truck comes a day, and that truck runs over the dog. It only takes one vehicle to shorten a dog's life.

Dogs often live to seven or eight years and then die of various diseases. It seems that if your Irish Terrier lives to eight years of age, your chances are good that you will have another two to six years with him. Eleven- and twelve-year-old Terriers are not unusual. The Fox Terrier I grew up with lived to 16 years of age. I was a youngster when she came to our house and she saw me through high school, college, and into marriage.

Cancer diagnosis can happen in any breed of dog and Irish Terriers are no exception. As in man, there is not always a cure, and early detection is your best form of prevention. Check your dog over each time you groom him for any lumps or bumps that you have not noticed before. Fast-growing lumps are cause for concern, particularly when found around the mammary glands. Any lump that you do not like the look of or is growing rapidly should be checked by your veterinarian.

Irish Terriers generally have a long life span. Keep your Irish Terrier healthy and in good shape to improve the quality of your life together.

GROOMING YOUR IRISH TERRIER

It's important to understand that when purchasing a dog, you have the responsibility of maintaining him. Think of it in terms of your child—you bathe your youngster, comb his hair, and put a clean set of clothes on him. The end product is that you have a child that smells good, looks nice, and that you enjoy having in your company. It is the same with your dog—keep the dog brushed, clean, and trimmed and you will find it a pleasure to be in his company.

The Irish is a double-coated dog. There is a dense, thick undercoat that protects the dog in all kinds of weather and there is a harsh outer coat. Coat care for the pet Irish can be much different and easier than the coat care for a show dog. The vast majority of Irish fanciers have a dog for a pet and they should not expect to maintain a show coat.

If you are planning to show your Irish Terrier, you will be ahead of the game if you purchase your puppy from a reputable breeder who grooms and shows her dogs. If so, this is the individual to see for grooming lessons on how to get your dog ready for the show ring. Grooming for the show is an art that cannot be learned in a few months. Furthermore, it is very difficult, but not impossible, to learn from a book.

John Sheehan of Firebrand Kennels has been raising Scottish Terriers for nearly 50 years and has bred, conditioned, and shown nine different Scots to the Best in Show spot. He learned to groom by watching others and then traveled to Seattle yearly to learn the finer points and finishing touches from Bob Bartos, one of the great old-time Scottie handlers. Therefore, it is not impossible for the novice to work himself up to competing on equal footing with the professional, but it does take time, effort, and the desire to want to learn and achieve.

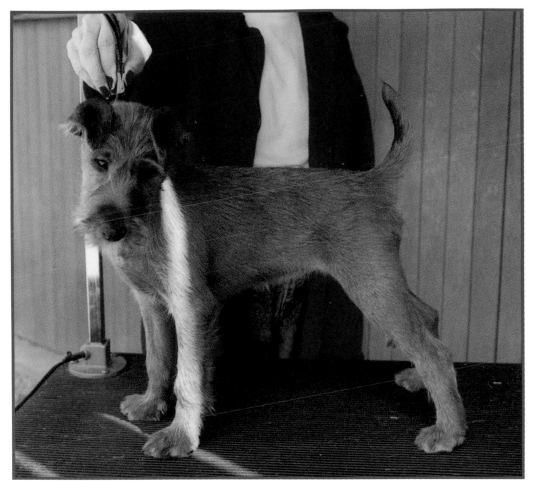

The primary difference between the pet and show Irish coat is that the show dog will have a dense undercoat with a shiny, harsh coat on top that will fit him like a jacket. With the proper coat, the dog presents a "smartness" in the ring that can be hard to beat. This coat can only be acquired by stripping the body coat with a stripping knife or stripping by hand. Within eight to ten weeks, and with the proper upkeep, he will have grown from his "underwear" outfit stage into a smart new outfit ready for the ring. This all takes skill, time, and interest in order to do it well.

Pet grooming is different from grooming for the show ring because you use a clipper on the body and scissors for trimming the furnishings. You will not have the harsh, tight-fitting jacket of the show Irish, but you will have a neat, clean, and trimmed dog that will still look like an Irish Terrier. Even those with kennels who are active in the show ring will clip their old dogs or those who are no longer being shown.

A grooming table, a metal comb, and electric clippers are just some of the necessary tools required to properly groom your Irish Terrier.

Here are the tools that you will need if you are going to do your own grooming:

1. A grooming table, something sturdy with a rubber mat covering the top. You will need a grooming arm, or a "hanger." (You can use a table in your laundry room with an eye hook in the ceiling for holding the leash.) Your dog will now be comfortable even if confined, and you will be able to work on the dog. Grooming is a very difficult and frustrating job if you try to groom without a table and a grooming arm.

2. A metal comb, a slicker brush, a good, sharp pair of scissors, and a toenail trimmer.

One way to groom your Irish Terrier's coat without losing the red tips of the hair shafts is to hand-strip the dog. Stripping not only retains his deep red color, but also his harsh, protective outer coat.

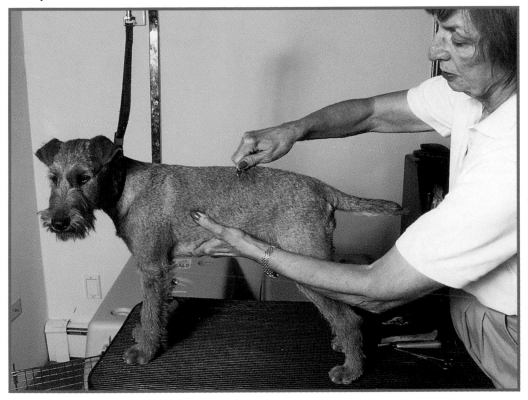

3. Electric clippers with a #10 blade.

One problem when clipping a coat is that you will lose the red tips of the hair shafts, which diminishes the red coat color. An option to clipping the coat is to hand-strip your dog. You will need a stripping knife, which can be purchased at a pet shop or at a dog show. Follow the same instructions as for clipping the coat, except instead of applying the clippers, you use the stripping knife. Stripping can be done every four to five months, and your dog will not only retain his deep red color, but also his harsh coat to protect him against dirt and water.

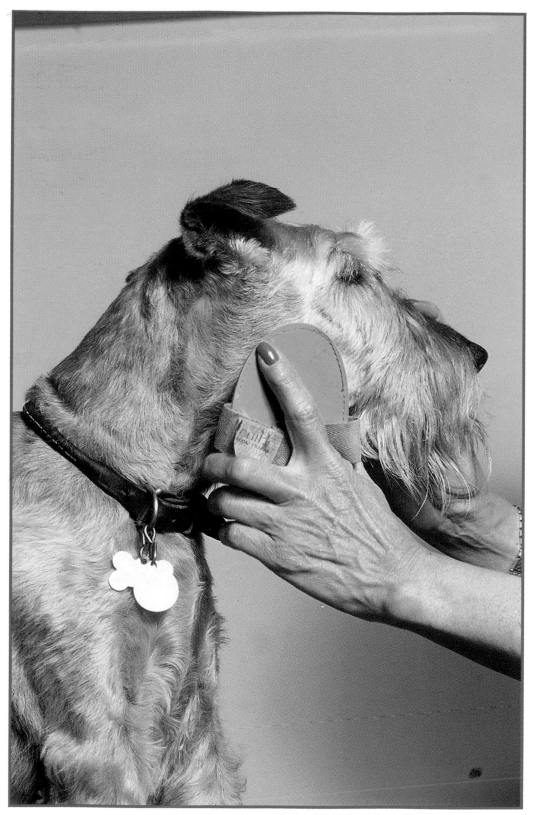

Opposite: Brushing your Irish Terrier once a week prevents matting and keeps your dog looking well maintained.

To start: Set your dog on the table and put the leash around his neck. Have your leash up behind his ears and pulled taut when you fasten it to your eyehook. Do not walk away and leave your dog unattended because he can jump off the table and be left dangling from the leash with his feet scrambling around in the air.

Take your slicker brush and brush out the entire coat. Brush the whiskers toward the nose, the body hair toward the tail, and the tail up toward the tip. Brush the leg furnishings up toward the body and brush the chest hair down toward the table. Hold the dog up by the front legs and gently brush the stomach hair, first toward the head and then back toward the rear. For cleanliness, you may want to take your scissors and trim the area around the penis. With the females, trim some of the hair around the vulva.

Now that your dog is brushed out, comb through the coat with your metal comb. By now a large amount of dead hair should be removed and your dog's appearance greatly improved. You may find some small mats and these can be worked out with your fingers or your comb. If you brush your dog out every week or so, you will not have too much of a problem with the mats.

We are now at the stage where you will take your clippers in hand. Look at the pictures of the Irish Terriers in this book and try to follow the pattern. There are also more comprehensive books on the Irish Terrier that will give pictorial grooming guides if you are interested in more specific guidelines. Your dog will only need to be clipped every three months or so, but you may want to touch up the head more often. Be sure to trim in the direction that the hair lies. Now take your comb and comb the leg hair down toward the table. Take your scissors and trim the legs neatly. The front legs should look like cylinders and the beard should have a squared-off look.

Take your scissors and trim off anything that sticks out. If this is your first experience, you may be a bit clumsy, but the hair will grow back in a short time. The finished product may not be quite what you had expected, but precision will come with experience and you will soon be very proud of your efforts. Your dog should now look like an Irish Terrier.

Put your dog in the laundry tub when you are finished and give him a good bath and rinsing. After toweling him down, return him to the grooming table

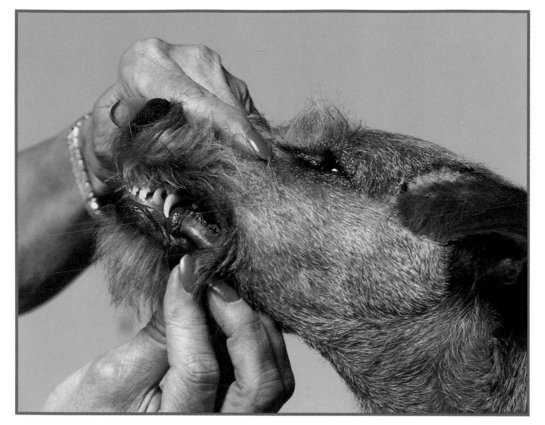

and trim the toenails on all four legs. At this point, you can dry your dog with a hair dryer and brush him out again, or you can let him dry naturally and then brush him out.

Clean, strong teeth are a sign of a healthy dog. Make sure to keep up with your Irish Terrier's dental needs.

If you have grooming problems, you can take your dog to the professional groomer for the first few times. The groomer will "set" the pattern and then it will be easier for you to get the Irish look by following the pattern that is already set in the coat. (Of course, you can eliminate all of the grooming for yourself, except for the weekly brushing, if you take your dog to the groomer every three months!) If the coat completely grows out before you start to groom, the pattern will be lost and then you will have to start over again. Just remember, many pet owners can do a much better job trimming their dogs than some professional groomers.

To wrap it up: Your pet should be brushed weekly and bathed as needed. Trim the toenails every month or so and plan to clip the dog every three months. Follow this plan and your dog will be clean, have a new "dress" every three months, and will look like a proper Irish Terrier!

YOUR PUPPY'S NEW HOME

It's a good decision to purchase the basic items you'll need before bringing your new puppy home. These adorable ten-week old Irish Terrier puppies would make a wonderful addition to any family. Owners, Paul and Peggy Gill.

Before actually collecting your puppy, it is better that you purchase the basic items you will need in advance of the pup's arrival date. This allows you more opportunity to shop around and ensure you have exactly what you want rather than having to buy lesser quality in a hurry.

It is always better to collect the puppy as early in the day as possible. In most instances this will mean that the puppy has a few hours with your family before it is time to retire for his first night's sleep away from his former home.

If the breeder is local, then you may not need any form of box to place the puppy in when you bring him home. A member of the family can hold the pup in his lap—duly protected by some towels just in case the puppy becomes car sick! Be sure to advise the breeder at what time you hope to arrive for the puppy, as this will obviously influence the feeding of the pup that morning or afternoon. If you arrive early in the day, then they will likely only give the pup a light breakfast so as to reduce the risk of travel sickness.

If the trip will be of a few hours duration, you should take a travel crate with you. The crate will provide your pup with a safe place to lie down and rest during the trip. During the trip, the puppy will no doubt wish to relieve his bowels, so you will have to make a few stops. On a long journey you may need a rest yourself, and can take the opportunity to let the puppy get some fresh air. However, do not let the puppy walk where there may have been a lot of other dogs because he might pick up an infection. Also, if he relieves his bowels at such a time, do not just leave the feces where they were dropped. This is the height of irre-sponsibility. It has resulted in many public parks and other places actually banning dogs. You can pur-chase poop-scoops from your pet shop and should have them with you whenever you are taking the dog out where he might foul a public place.

Your journey home should be made as quickly as possible. If it is a hot day, be sure the car interior is amply supplied with fresh air. It should never be too hot or too cold for the puppy. The pup must never be placed where he might be subject to a draft. If the journey requires an overnight stop at a motel, be aware that other guests will not appreciate a puppy crying half the night. You must regard the puppy as a baby and comfort him so he does not cry for long periods. The worst thing you can do is to shout at or smack him. This will mean your relationship is off to a really bad start. You wouldn't smack a baby, and your puppy is still very much just this.

ON ARRIVING HOME

By the time you arrive home the puppy may be very tired, in which case he should be taken to his sleeping area and allowed to rest. Children should not be allowed to interfere with the pup when he is sleeping. If the pup is not tired, he can be allowed to investigate his new home—but always under

This little puppy is having a slumber party. Puppies require a lot of sleep in the first few weeks of their arrival. Owners, Bruce and Nancy Petersen.

your close supervision. After a short look around, the puppy will no doubt appreciate a light meal and a drink of water. Do not overfeed him at his first meal because he will be in an excited state and more likely to be sick.

Although it is an obvious temptation, you should not invite friends and neighbors around to see the new arrival until he has had at least 48 hours in which to settle down. Indeed, if you can delay this longer then do so, especially if the puppy is not fully vaccinated. At the very least, the visitors might introduce some local bacteria on their clothing that the puppy is not immune to. This aspect is always a risk when a pup has been moved some distance, so the fewer people the pup meets in the first week or so the better.

DANGERS IN THE HOME

Your home holds many potential dangers for a little mischievous puppy, so you must think about these in advance and be sure he is protected from them. The more obvious are as follows:

Open Fires. All open fires should be protected by a mesh screen guard so there is no danger of the pup being burned by spitting pieces of coal or wood.

Electrical Wires. Puppies just love chewing on things, so be sure that all electrical appliances are neatly hidden from view and are not left plugged in when not in use. It is not sufficient simply to turn the plug switch to the off position—pull the plug from the socket.

Open Doors. A door would seem a pretty innocuous object, yet with a strong draft it could kill or injure a puppy easily if it is slammed shut. Always ensure there is no risk of this happening. It is most likely during warm weather when you have windows or outside doors open and a sudden gust of wind blows through.

Balconies. If you live in a high-rise building, obviously the pup must be protected from falling. Be sure he cannot get through any railings on your patio, balcony, or deck.

Ponds and Pools. A garden pond or a swimming pool is a very dangerous place for a little puppy to be near. Be sure it is well screened so there is no risk of the pup falling in. It takes barely a minute for a pup—or a child—to drown.

The Kitchen. While many puppies will be kept in the kitchen, at least while they are toddlers and not able to control their bowel movements, this is a room full of danger—especially while you are cooking. When cooking, keep the puppy in a play pen or in another room where he is safely out of harm's way. Alternatively, if you have a carry box or crate, put him in this so he can still see you but is well protected.

Be aware, when using washing machines, that more than one puppy has clambered in and decided to have a nap and received a wash instead! If you leave the washing machine door open and leave the room for any reason, then be sure to check inside the machine before you close the door and switch on.

Small Children. Toddlers and small children should never be left unsupervised with puppies. In spite of such advice it is amazing just how many people not only do this but also allow children to pull and maul

Newborn puppies are very vulnerable, so take all the necessary precautions to protect his health and well-being.

Children need to be taught the correct way to hold a puppy. If they are not careful, the pup can be seriously injured.

pups. They should be taught from the outset that a puppy is not a plaything to be dragged about the home—and they should be promptly scolded if they disobey.

Children must be shown how to lift a puppy so it is safe. Failure by you to correctly educate your children about dogs could one day result in their getting a very nasty bite or scratch. When a puppy is lifted, his weight must always be supported. To lift the pup, first place your right hand under his chest. Next, secure the pup by using your left hand to hold his neck. Now you can lift him and bring him close to your chest. Never lift a pup by his ears and, while he can be lifted by the scruff of his neck where the fur is loose, there is no reason ever to do this, so don't.

Beyond the dangers already cited you may be able to think of other ones that are specific to your home—steep basement steps or the like. Go around your home and check out all potential problems—you'll be glad you did.

THE FIRST NIGHT

The first few nights a puppy spends away from his mother and littermates are quite traumatic for him. He will feel very lonely, maybe cold, and will certainly miss the heartbeat of his siblings when sleeping. To help overcome his loneliness it may help to place a clock next to his bed—one with a loud tick. This will in some way soothe him, as the clock ticks to a rhythm not dissimilar from a heart beat. A cuddly toy may also help in the first few weeks. A dim nightlight may

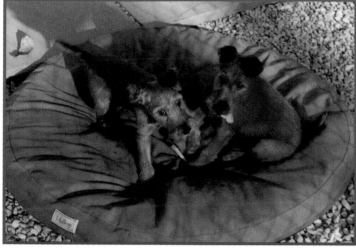

A puppy's first night in a new home can be difficult because he may miss his littermates. Pay him extra attention until he gets adjusted.

provide some comfort to the puppy, because his eyes will not yet be fully able to see in the dark. The puppy may want to leave his bed for a drink or to relieve himself.

If the pup does whimper in the night, there are two things you should not do. One is to get up and chastise him, because he will not understand why you are shouting at him; and the other is to rush to comfort him every time he cries because he will quickly realize that if he wants you to come running all he needs to do is to holler loud enough!

By all means give your puppy some extra attention on his first night, but after this quickly refrain from so doing. The pup will cry for a while but then settle down and go to sleep. Some pups are, of course, worse than others in this respect, so you must use balanced judgment in the matter. Many owners take their pups to bed with them, and there is certainly nothing wrong with this.

The pup will be no trouble in such cases. However, you should only do this if you intend to let this be a permanent arrangement, otherwise it is hardly fair to the puppy. If you have decided to have two puppies, then they will keep each other company and you will have few problems.

OTHER PETS

If you have other pets in the home then the puppy must be introduced to them under careful supervision. Puppies will get on just fine with any other pets—but you must make due allowance for the respective sizes of the pets concerned, and appreciate that your puppy has a rather playful nature. It would be very foolish to leave him with a young rabbit. The pup will want to play and might bite the bunny and get altogether too rough with it. Kittens are more able to defend themselves from overly cheeky pups, who will get a quick scratch if they overstep the mark. The adult cat could obviously give the pup a very bad scratch, though generally cats will jump clear of pups and watch them from a suitable vantage point. Eventually they will meet at ground level where the cat will quickly hiss and box a puppy's ears. The pup will soon learn to respect an adult cat; thereafter they will probably develop into great friends as the pup matures into an adult dog.

HOUSETRAINING

Undoubtedly, the first form of training your puppy will undergo is in respect to his toilet habits. To achieve this you can use either newspaper, or a large litter tray filled with soil or lined with newspaper. A puppy cannot control his bowels until he is a few months old, and not fully until he is an adult. Therefore you must anticipate his needs and be prepared for a few accidents. The prime times a pup will urinate and defecate are shortly after he wakes up from a sleep, shortly after he has eaten, and after he has been playing awhile. He will usually whimper and start searching the room for a suitable place. You must quickly pick him up and place him on the newspaper or in the litter tray. Hold him in position gently but firmly. He might jump

Mischievous and curious, puppies are notorious for exploring in unknown places. Keep a close eye on your Irish Terrier pup to make sure he stays out of trouble.

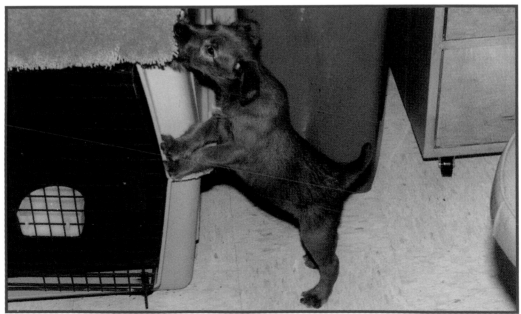

Providing your puppy with various toys will keep him occupied and happy.

out of the box without doing anything on the first one or two occasions, but if you simply repeat the procedure every time you think he wants to relieve himself then eventually he will get the message.

When he does defecate as required, give him plenty of praise, telling him what a good puppy he is. The litter tray or newspaper must, of course, be cleaned or replaced after each use—puppies do not like using a dirty toilet any more than you do. The pup's toilet can be placed near the kitchen door and as he gets older the tray can be placed outside while the door is open. The pup will then start to use it while he is outside. From that time on, it is easy to get the pup to use a given area of the yard.

Many breeders recommend the popular alternative of crate training. Upon bringing the pup home, introduce him to his crate. The open wire crate is the best choice, placed in a restricted, draft-free area of the home. Put the pup's Nylabone® and other favorite toys in the crate along with a wool blanket or other suitable bedding. The puppy's natural cleanliness instincts prohibit him from soiling in the place where he sleeps, his crate. The puppy should be allowed to go in and out of the open crate during the day, but he should sleep in the crate at the night and at other intervals during the day. Whenever the pup is taken out of his crate, he should be brought outside (or to his newspapers) to do his business. Never use the crate as a place of punishment. You will see how quickly your pup takes to his crate, considering it as his own safe haven from the big world around him.

THE EARLY DAYS

You will no doubt be given much advice on how to bring up your puppy. This will come from dog-owning friends, neighbors, and through articles and books you may read on the subject. Some of the advice will be sound, some will be nothing short of rubbish. What you should do above all else is to keep an open mind and let common sense prevail over prejudice and worn-out ideas that have been handed down over the centuries. There is no one way that is superior to all others, no more than there is no one dog that is exactly a replica of another. Each is an individual and must always be regarded as such.

A dog never becomes disobedient, unruly, or a menace to society without the full consent of his owner. Your puppy may have many limitations, but the singular biggest limitation he is confronted with in so many instances is his owner's inability to understand his needs and how to cope with them.

IDENTIFICATION

It is a sad reflection on our society that the number of dogs and cats stolen every year runs into many thousands. To these can be added the number that get lost. If you do not want your cherished pet to be lost or stolen, then you should see that he is carrying a permanent identification number, as well as a temporary tag on his collar.

Permanent markings come in the form of tattoos placed either inside the pup's ear flap, or on the inner side of a pup's upper rear leg. The number given is then recorded with one of the national registration companies. Research laboratories will not purchase dogs carrying numbers as they realize these are clearly someone's pet, and not abandoned animals. As a result, thieves will normally abandon dogs so marked and this at least gives the dog a chance to be taken to the police or the dog pound, when the number can be traced and the dog reunited with its family. The only problem with this method at this time is that there are a number of registration bodies, so it is not always apparent which one the dog is registered with (as you

Opposite: These two mischievous Irish Terriers aren't giving away their full identity, but they do look like they are planning an escape. Carefully supervise your dog when outside.

provide the actual number). However, each registration body is aware of his competitors and will normally be happy to supply their addresses. Those holding the dog can check out which one you are with. It is not a perfect system, but until such is developed it's the best available.

Another permanent form of identification is the microchip, a computer chip that is injected between the dog's shoulder blades. The dog feels no discomfort. The dog also receives a tag that says he is microchipped. If the dog is lost and picked up by the humane society, they can trace the owner by scanning the microchip. It is the safest form of identification.

A temporary tag takes the form of a metal or plastic disk large enough for you to place the dog's name and your phone number on it—maybe even your address as well. In virtually all places you will be required to obtain a license for your puppy. This may not become applicable until the pup is six months old, but it might apply regardless of his age. Much depends upon the state within a country, or the country itself, so check with your veterinarian if the breeder has not already advised you on this.

Proper identification tags will help to ensure your Irish Terrier will be returned should you become separated.

FEEDING YOUR IRISH TERRIER

Dog owners today are fortunate in that they live in an age when considerable cash has been invested in the study of canine nutritional requirements. This means dog food manufacturers are very concerned about ensuring that their foods are of the best quality. The result of all of their studies, apart from the food itself, is that dog owners are bombarded with advertisements telling them why they must purchase a given brand. The number of products available to you is unlimited, so it is hardly surprising to find that dogs in general suffer from obesity and an excess of vitamins, rather than the reverse. Be sure to feed age-appropriate food—puppy food up to one year of age, adult food thereafter. Generally breeders recommend dry food supplemented by canned, if needed.

Providing your Irish Terrier with the proper nutrients is vital to his overall health. A mother's milk carries all of the necessary vitamins needed for a puppy to grow into a strong adult.

Puppies need a balance of protein, fat, and carbohydrates in their diet, as well as vitamins, minerals and plenty of water.

FACTORS AFFECTING NUTRITIONAL NEEDS

Activity Level. A dog that lives in a country environment and is able to exercise for long periods of the day will need more food than the same breed of dog living in an apartment and given little exercise.

Quality of the Food. Obviously the quality of food will affect the quantity required by a puppy. If the nutritional content of a food is low then the puppy will need more of it than if a better quality food was fed.

Balance of Nutrients and Vitamins. Feeding a puppy the correct balance of nutrients is not easy because the average person is not able to measure out ratios of one to another, so it is a case of trying to see that nothing is in excess. However, only tests, or your veterinarian, can be the source of reliable advice.

Genetic and Biological Variation. Apart from all of the other considerations, it should be remembered that each puppy is an individual. His genetic make-up will influence not only his physical characteristics but also his metabolic efficiency. This being so, two pups from the same litter can vary quite a bit in the amount of food they need to perform the same function under the same conditions. If you consider the potential combinations of all of these factors then you will see that pups of a given breed could vary quite a bit in the amount of food they will need. Before discussing feeding quantities it is valuable to know at least a little about the composition of food and its role in the body.

COMPOSITION AND ROLE OF FOOD

The main ingredients of food are protein, fats, and carbohydrates, each of which is needed in relatively large quantities when compared to the other needs of vitamins and minerals. The other vital ingredient of food is, of course, water. Although all foods obviously contain some of the basic ingredients needed for an animal to survive, they do not all contain the ingredients in the needed ratios or type. For example, there are many forms of protein, just as there are many types of carbohydrates. Both of these compounds are found in meat and in vegetable matter—but not all of those that are needed will be in one particular meat or vegetable. Plants, especially, do not contain certain amino acids that are required for the synthesis of certain proteins needed by dogs.

Likewise, vitamins are found in meats and vegetable matter, but vegetables are a richer source of most. Meat contains very little carbohydrates. Some vitamins can be synthesized by the dog, so do not need to be supplied via the food. Dogs are carnivores and this means their digestive tract has evolved to need a high quantity of meat as compared to humans. The digestive system of carnivores is unable to break down the tough cellulose walls of plant matter, but it is easily able to assimilate proteins from meat.

In order to gain its needed vegetable matter in a form that it can cope with, the carnivore eats all of its prey. This includes the partly digested food

POP pups™ are 100 percent edible and contain no salt, sugar, alcohol, or preservatives.

within the stomach. In commercially prepared foods, the cellulose is broken down by cooking. During this process the vitamin content is either greatly reduced or lost altogether. The manufacturer therefore adds vitamins once the heat process has been completed. This is why commercial foods are so useful as part of a feeding regimen, providing they are of good quality and from a company that has prepared the foods very carefully.

Proteins

These are made from amino acids, of which at least ten are essential if a puppy is to maintain healthy growth. Proteins provide the building blocks for the puppy's body. The richest sources are meat, fish and poultry, together with their by-products. The latter will include milk, cheese, yogurt, fishmeal, and eggs. Vegetable matter that has a high protein content includes soy beans, together with numerous corn and other plant extracts that have been dehydrated. The actual protein content needed in the diet will be determined both by the activity level of the dog and his age. The total protein need will also be influenced by the digestibility factor of the food given.

Fats serve many roles in your puppy's diet. They provide insulation, protect the organs, and offer the richest source of energy. "Kerri" owned by Stephen Skolnik is the perfect example of what a seven-week-old puppy should look like.

MADE WITH
REAL CARROTS

BONE-HARD
HEALTH CHEW
FIGHTS OBESITY AND
TOOTH PLAQUE

NYLABONE

Carrot
-BONE™

100% NATURAL INGREDIENTS
NO ADDED SALT, SUGAR, COLOR ADDITIVES OR PRESERVATIVES

MADE IN THE USA

NCB-102 REGULAR SIZE
Net Weight: 1.1 oz. / 30 grams

The CarrotBone™ by Nylabone® is a durable chew that can be served to yor Irish Terrier as is or microwaved to a biscuit consistency.

Fats

These serve numerous roles in the puppy's body. They provide insulation against the cold, and help buffer the organs from knocks and general activity shocks. They provide the richest source of energy, and reserves of this, and they are vital in the transport of vitamins and other nutrients, via the blood, to all other organs. Finally, it is the fat content within a diet that gives it palatability. It is important that the fat content of a diet should not be excessive. This is because the high energy content of fats (more than twice that of protein or carbohydrate) will increase the overall energy content of the diet. The puppy will adjust its food intake to that of its energy needs, which are obviously more easily met in a high-energy diet. This will mean that while the fats are providing the energy needs of the puppy, the over-all diet may not be providing its protein, vitamin, and mineral needs, so signs of protein deficiency will become apparent. Rich sources of fats are meat, their byproducts (butter, milk), and vegetable oils, such as safflower, olive, corn or soy bean.

Carbohydrates

These are the principal energy compounds given to puppies and adult dogs. Their inclusion within most commercial brand dog foods is for cost, rather than dietary needs. These compounds are more commonly known as sugars, and they are seen in simple or complex compounds of carbon, hydrogen, and oxygen.

One of the simple sugars is called glucose, and it is vital to many metabolic processes. When large chains of glucose are created, they form compound sugars. One of these is called glycogen, and it is found in the cells of animals. Another, called starch, is the material that is found in the cells of plants.

Vitamins

These are not foods as such but chemical compounds that assist in all aspects of an animal's life. They help in so many ways that to attempt to describe these effectively would require a chapter in itself. Fruits are a rich source of vitamins, as is the liver of most animals. Many vitamins are unstable and easily destroyed by light, heat, moisture, or rancidity. An excess of vitamins, especially A and D, has been proven to be very harmful. Provided a puppy is receiving a balanced diet, it is most unlikely there will be a deficiency, whereas hypervitaminosis (an excess of vitamins) has become quite common due to owners and breeders feeding unneeded supplements. The only time you should feed extra vitamins to your puppy is if your veterinarian advises you to.

Not only is water refreshing, it is the most important nutrient of all. Always keep your Irish Terrier supplied with fresh, clean water.

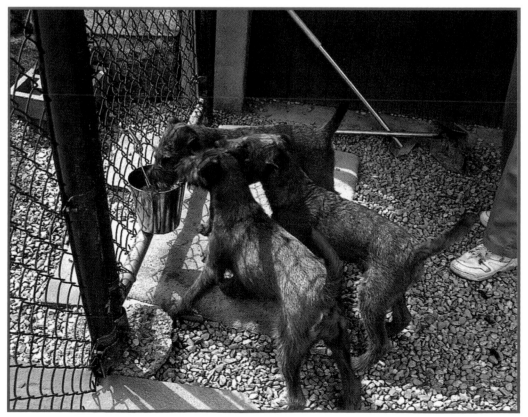

Minerals

These provide strength to bone and cell tissue, as well as assist in many metabolic processes. Examples are calcium, phosphorous, copper, iron, magnesium, selenium, potassium, zinc, and sodium. The recommended amounts of all minerals in the diet has not been fully established. Calcium and phosphorous are known to be important, especially to puppies. They help in forming strong bone. As with vitamins, a mineral deficiency is most unlikely in pups given a good and varied diet. Again, an excess can create problems—this applying equally to calcium.

Opposite: Adhering to a feeding schedule can help you monitor your dog's health and keep him from snacking in between meals.

Water

This is the most important of all nutrients, as is easily shown by the fact that the adult dog is made up of about 60 percent water, the puppy containing an even higher percentage. Dogs must retain a water balance, which means that the total intake should be balanced by the total output. The intake comes either by direct input (the tap or its equivalent), plus water released when food is oxidized, known as metabolic water (remember that all foods

It's a very happy, healthy birthday for this adorable duo.

contain the elements hydrogen and oxygen that recombine in the body to create water). A dog without adequate water will lose condition more rapidly than one depleted of food, a fact common to most animal species.

AMOUNT TO FEED

The best way to determine dietary requirements is by observing the puppy's general health and physical appearance. If he is well covered with flesh, shows good bone development and muscle, and is an active alert puppy, then his diet is fine. A puppy will consume about twice as much as an adult (of the same breed). You should ask the breeder of your puppy to show you the amounts fed to their pups and this will be a good starting point.

The puppy should eat his meal in about five to seven minutes. Any leftover food can be discarded or placed into the refrigerator until the next meal (but be sure it is thawed fully if your fridge is very cold).

If the puppy quickly devours its meal and is clearly still hungry, then you are not giving him enough food. If he eats readily but then begins to pick at it, or walks away leaving a quantity, then you are probably giving him too much food. Adjust this at the next meal and you will quickly begin to appreciate what the correct amount is. If, over a number of weeks, the pup starts to look fat, then he is obviously overeating; the reverse is true if he starts to look thin compared with others of the same breed.

WHEN TO FEED

It really does not matter what times of the day the puppy is fed, as long as he receives the needed quantity of food. Puppies from 8 weeks to 12 or 16 weeks need 3 or 4 meals a day. Older puppies and adult dogs should be fed twice a day. What is most important is that the feeding times are reasonably regular. They can be tailored to fit in with your own timetable—for example, 7 a.m. and 6 p.m. The dog will then expect his meals at these times each day. Keeping regular feeding times and feeding set amounts will help you monitor your puppy's or dog's health. If a dog that's normally enthusiastic about mealtimes and eats readily suddenly shows a lack of interest in food, you'll know something's not right.

TRAINING YOUR IRISH TERRIER

Once your puppy has settled into your home and responds to his name, then you can begin his basic training. Before giving advice on how you should go about doing this, two important points should be made. You should train the puppy in isolation of any potential distractions, and you should keep all lessons very short. It is essential that you have the full attention of your puppy. This is not possible if there are other people about, or televisions and radios on,

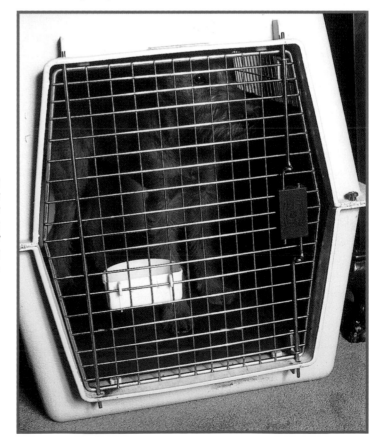

You should begin training your Irish Terrier puppy as soon as he settles into his new home. Crate training is just one of the many parts of the training process.

or other pets in the vicinity. Even when the pup has become a young adult, the maximum time you should allocate to a lesson is about 20 minutes. However, you can give the puppy more than one lesson a day, three being as many as are recommended, each well spaced apart.

Before beginning a lesson, always play a little game with the puppy so he is in an active state of mind and thus more receptive to the matter at hand. Likewise, always end a lesson with fun-time for the pup, and always—this is most important—end on a high note, praising the puppy. Let the lesson end when the pup has done as you require so he receives lots of fuss. This will really build his confidence.

COLLAR AND LEASH TRAINING

Training a puppy to his collar and leash is very easy. Place a collar on the puppy and, although he will initially try to bite at it, he will soon forget it, the more so if you play with him. You can leave the collar on for a few hours. Some people leave their dogs' collars on all of the time, others only when they are taking the dog out. If it is to be left on, purchase a narrow or round one so it does not mark the fur.

Once the puppy ignores his collar, then you can attach the leash to it and let the puppy pull this along behind it for a few minutes. However, if the pup starts to chew at the leash, simply hold the leash but keep it slack and let the pup go where he wants. The idea is to let him get the feel of the leash, but not get in the habit of chewing it. Repeat this a couple of times a day for two days and the pup will get used to the leash without thinking that it will restrain him—which you will not have attempted to do yet.

Next, you can let the pup understand that the leash will restrict his movements. The first time he realizes this, he will pull and buck or just sit down. Immediately call the pup to you and give him lots of fuss. Never tug on the leash so the puppy is dragged along the floor, as this simply implants a negative thought in his mind.

THE COME COMMAND

Come is the most vital of all commands and especially so for the independently minded dog. To teach the puppy to come, let him reach the end of a long lead, then give the command and his name, gently pulling him toward you at the same time. As soon as

Opposite: It shouldn't take long before a puppy gets used to his leash and collar.

Love and affection are the two most important things a puppy needs to grow into a well-adjusted adult. This precious 12-week-old Irish Terrier has found the perfect lap to rest in.

he associates the word come with the action of moving toward you, pull only when he does not respond immediately. As he starts to come, move back to make him learn that he must come from a distance as well as when he is close to you. Soon you may be able to practice without a leash, but if he is slow to come or notably disobedient, go to him and pull him toward you, repeating the command. Never scold a dog during this exercise—or any other exercise. Remember the trick is that the puppy must want to come to you. For the very independent dog, hand signals may work better than verbal commands.

THE SIT COMMAND

As with most basic commands, your puppy will learn this one in just a few lessons. You can give the puppy two lessons a day on the sit command but he will make just as much progress with one 15-minute lesson each day. Some trainers will advise you that you should not proceed to other commands until the previous one has been learned really well. However,

Opposite: In order to compete in a show, your Irish Terrier must be well trained and obedient.

a bright young pup is quite capable of handling more than one command per lesson, and certainly per day. Indeed, as time progresses, you will be going through each command as a matter of routine before a new one is attempted. This is so the puppy always starts, as well as ends, a lesson on a high note, having successfully completed something.

Call the puppy to you and fuss over him. Place one hand on his hindquarters and the other under his upper chest. Say "Sit" in a pleasant (never harsh) voice. At the same time, push down his rear end and push up under his chest. Now lavish praise on the puppy. Repeat this a few times and your pet will get the idea. Once the puppy is in the sit position you will release your hands. At first he will tend to get up, so immediately repeat the exercise. The lesson will end when the pup is in the sit position. When the puppy understands the command, and does it right away, you can slowly move backwards so that you are a few feet away from him. If he attempts to come to you, simply place him back in the original position and start again. Do not attempt to keep the pup in the sit position for too long. At this age, even a few seconds is a long while and you do not want him to get bored with lessons before he has even begun them.

THE HEEL COMMAND

All dogs should be able to walk nicely on a leash without their owners being involved in a tug-of-war. The heel command will follow leash training. Heel training is best done where you have a wall to one side of you. This will restrict the puppy's lateral movements, so you only have to contend with forward and backward situations. A fence is an alternative, or you can do the lesson in the garage. Again, it is better to do the lesson in private, not on a public sidewalk where there will be many distractions.

With a puppy, there will be no need to use a choke collar as you can be just as effective with a regular one. The leash should be of good length, certainly not too short. You can adjust the space between you, the puppy, and the wall so your pet has only a small amount of room to move sideways. This being so, he will either hang back or pull ahead—the latter is the more desirable state as it indicates a bold pup who is not frightened of you.

Hold the leash in your right hand and pass it through

your left. As the puppy moves ahead and strains on the leash, give the leash a quick jerk backwards with your left hand, at the same time saying "Heel." The position you want the pup to be in is such that his chest is level with, or just behind, an imaginary line from your knee. When the puppy is in this position, praise him and begin walking again, and the whole exercise will be repeated. Once the puppy begins to get the message, you can use your left hand to pat the side of your knee so the pup is encouraged to keep close to your side.

It is useful to suddenly do an about-turn when the pup understands the basics. The puppy will now be behind you, so you can pat your knee and say "Heel." As soon as the pup is in the correct position, give him lots of praise. The puppy will now be beginning to associate certain words with certain actions. Whenever he is not in the heel position he will experience displeasure as you jerk the leash, but when he comes alongside you he will receive praise. Given these two options, he will always prefer the latter—assuming he has no other reason to fear you, which would then create a dilemma in his mind.

Once the lesson has been well learned, then you can adjust your pace from a slow walk to a quick one and the puppy will come to adjust. The slow walk is always the more difficult for most puppies, as they are usually anxious to be on the move.

If you have no wall to walk against then things will be a little more difficult because the pup will tend to wander to his left. This means you need to give lateral jerks as well as bring the pup to your side. End the lesson when the pup is walking nicely beside you. Begin the lesson with a few sit commands (which he understands by now), so you're starting with success and praise. If your puppy is nervous on the leash, you should never drag him to your side as you may see so many other people do (who obviously didn't invest in a good book like you did!). If the pup sits down, call him to your side and give lots of praise. The pup must always come to you because he wants to. If he is dragged to your side he will see you doing the dragging—a big negative. When he races ahead he does not see you jerk the leash, so all he knows is that something restricted his movement and, once he was in a given position, you gave him lots of praise. This is using canine psychology to your advantage.

Always try to remember that if a dog must be disciplined, then try not to let him associate the

Opposite: Although the down command can be one of the more difficult ones to learn and accept, pretty "Casey" practices it with ease.

discipline with you. This is not possible in all matters but, where it is, this is definitely to be preferred.

THE STAY COMMAND

This command follows from the sit. Face the puppy and say "Sit." Now step backwards, and as you do, say "Stay." Let the pup remain in the position for only a few seconds before calling him to you and giving lots of praise. Repeat this, but step further back. You do not need to shout at the puppy. Your pet is not deaf; in fact, his hearing is far better than yours. Speak just loudly enough for the pup to hear, yet use a firm voice. You can stretch the word to form a "sta-a-a-y." If the pup gets up and comes to you simply lift him up, place him back in the original position, and start again. As the pup comes to understand the command, you can move further and further back.

The next test is to walk away after placing the pup. This will mean your back is to him, which will tempt him to follow you. Keep an eye over your shoulder, and the minute the pup starts to move, spin around and, using a sterner voice, say either "Sit" or "Stay." If the pup has gotten quite close to you, then, again, return him to the original position.

As the weeks go by you can increase the length of time the pup is left in the stay position—but two to three minutes is quite long enough for a puppy. If your puppy drops into a lying position and is clearly more comfortable, there is nothing wrong with this. Likewise, your pup will want to face the direction in which you walked off. Some trainers will insist that the dog faces the direction he was placed in, regardless of whether you move off on his blind side. I have never believed in this sort of obedience because it has no practical benefit.

THE DOWN COMMAND

From the puppy's viewpoint, the down command can be one of the more difficult ones to accept. This is because the position is one taken up by a submissive dog in a wild pack situation. A timid dog will roll over—a natural gesture of submission. A bolder pup will want to get up, and might back off, not feeling he should have to submit to this command. He will feel that he is under attack from you and about to be punished—which is what would be the position in his natural environment. Once he comes to understand this is not the case, he will accept this unnatural position without any problem.

You may notice that some dogs will sit very quickly, but will respond to the down command more slowly—it is their way of saying that they will obey the command, but under protest!

There two ways to teach this command. One is, in my mind, more intimidating than the other, but it is up to you to decide which one works best for you. The first method is to stand in front of your puppy and bring him to the sit position, with his collar and leash on. Pass the leash under your left foot so that when you pull on it, the result is that the pup's neck is forced downwards. With your free left hand, push the pup's shoulders down while at the same time saying "Down." This is when a bold pup will instantly try to back off and wriggle in full protest. Hold the pup firmly by the shoulders so he stays in the position for a second or two, then tell him what a good dog he is and give him lots of praise. Repeat this only a few times in a lesson because otherwise the puppy will get bored and upset over this command. End with an easy command that brings back the pup's confidence.

The second method, and the one I prefer, is done as follows: Stand in front of the pup and then tell him to sit. Now kneel down, which is immediately far less intimidating to the puppy than to have you towering above him. Take each of his front legs and pull them forward, at the same time saying "Down." Release the legs and quickly apply light pressure on the shoulders with your left hand. Then, as quickly, say "Good boy" and give lots of fuss. Repeat two or three times only. The pup will learn over a few lessons. Remember, this is a very submissive act on the pup's behalf, so there is no need to rush matters.

RECALL TO HEEL COMMAND

When your puppy is coming to the heel position from an off-leash situation—such as if he has been running free—he should do this in the correct manner. He should pass behind you and take up his position and then sit. To teach this command, have the pup in front of you in the sit position with his collar and leash on. Hold the leash in your right hand. Give him the command to heel, and pat your left knee. As the pup starts to move forward, use your right hand to guide him behind you. If need be you can hold his collar and walk the dog around the back of you to the desired position. You will need to repeat this a few times until the dog understands what is wanted.

When he has done this a number of times, you can try it without the collar and leash. If the pup comes up toward your left side, then bring him to the sit position in front of you, hold his collar and walk him around the back of you. He will eventually understand and automatically pass around your back each time. If the dog is already behind you when you recall him, then he should automatically come to your left side, which you will be patting with your hand.

THE NO COMMAND

This is a command that must be obeyed every time without fail. There are no halfway stages, he must be 100-percent reliable. Most delinquent dogs have never been taught this command; included in these are the jumpers, the barkers, and the biters. Were your puppy to approach a poisonous snake or any other potential danger, the no command, coupled with the recall, could save his life. You do not need to give a specific lesson for this command because it will crop up time and again in day-to-day life.

These two buddies look like they're enjoying a little roughhousing. If they're not careful, they could be hearing the "No" command very soon.

If the puppy is chewing a slipper, you should approach the pup, take hold of the slipper, and say "No" in a stern voice. If he jumps onto the furniture, lift him off and say "No" and place him gently on the floor. You must be consistent in the use of the command and apply it every time he is doing something you do not want him to do.

KEEPING THE IRISH TERRIER BUSY

Every Irish Terrier should be able to lie around the house, have a good meal, receive love and attention, and be taken for a walk or a romp every day. However, some owners like the challenge of working with their dog, training him to follow commands, and seeing him perform the chores that he was bred to do. With terriers, an owner can work in obedience, including tracking or utility, or train in agility. It is surely a challenge to work a terrier, but it can be done, and an owner can have a tremendous feeling of accomplishment once a goal is set and reached.

Because of their high degree of intelligence and independent spirit, Irish Terriers can be trained to participate in many different activities.

Terriers are not an easy breed to work with in obedience because with their intelligence and independent spirit, they can sometimes be more difficult to train than anticipated. You will see an abundance of Golden Retrievers, Poodles, and Miniature Schnauzers in obedience classes because these are breeds that are easy to work with. Not only are they intelligent, but more importantly, they have a willingness to please their master. The Irish Terrier is easily distracted and busy, but he is an intelligent dog and he does respond to training. Of course, when training a smart and independent dog, the handler will often learn humility while the dog is learning his sits and stays. For obedience work, dog and handler need aptitude and determination. The handler must take time to work his dog every day, even if it is only for five minutes or so. The handler must also have patience, and the dog must have a desire to perform and at least some willingness to please. Once this match is made, a handler and his dog can be well on their way toward an obedience degree, and the handler will feel a tremendous amount of achievement and accomplishment to have such a smart dog working by his side. Spectators at a dog show love to watch the obedience rings because they can understand what the dog is doing (or not doing) better than when they watch the conformation rings. The first Irish Terrier earned a Companion Degree in 1936. In 1938, Ch. No Retreat was the first AKC champion to earn not only a Companion Degree (CD) but his Companion Degree Excellent (CDX). In 1949, Crashmore was the first to earn his Utility Degree (UD). Ch. Greenbriar Fiddler, UDT, not only earned his AKC championship and his Utility Degree, but was also the first in the breed to earn a Tracking title—a wonderful achievement for a dog of any breed.

From 1936 through 1989, there were a total of 156 Companion Degrees, 40 CDXs, 8 Utility Degrees, and 3 Tracking titles earned in the breed, proving that although the Irish may not be easy to train, it can be done with a patient and persistent handler and a willing dog.

Obedience classes are offered throughout the country and unless you live in a very remote area, your town or city should offer you a selection of training clubs. Some classes are offered by private individuals, others by obedience clubs or all-breed clubs. There are different methods of instruction and you

may find it worthwhile to visit various classes to see which method of training you prefer.

The Irish Terrier has been said to have a fractious personality, not quick to pick a fight but eager to hold his ground when pushed by another animal, particularly another dog. He stops at no challenge. Therefore, it is often a good idea to start your dog in obedience while he is still a pup. You may only need to take the beginning classes, which are about six lessons in six weeks of training. By then, you will have a well-mannered gentleman by your side who will come when called and stay put when told to do so. A. Croxton Smith wrote, "Dogs that are very game are usually surly or snappish. The Irish Terrier as a breed is an exception, being remarkably good-tempered, notably so with mankind; however, he is a little too

Keeping your Irish Terrier occupied not only makes your life easier, but benefits the dog's physical health as well. This agile Irish Terrier clears the high jump with ease and precision.

ready to resent interference on the part of other dogs. There is a heedless, reckless pluck about the Irish Terrier which is characteristic, and coupled with the headlong dash, blind to all consequences, with which he rushes at his adversary, has earned for the breed the proud epithet of 'the daredevils.' On occasion they can prove they have the courage of a lion and will fight unto the last breath in their bodies." James Spencer wrote in a *Dog Fancy* article on Irish breeds, "An Irish Terrier doesn't just look you in the eye; it challenges you. This is the Jimmy Cagney of terriers: cocky, aggressive, agile, quick, alert, athletic. If another dog—of any size—would care to go a couple of rounds, the Irish Terrier will oblige. If any stranger fails to show proper respect for the Irish Terrier's turf and folks, said stranger will experience the fury of the little dog's teeth with little time wasted on ceremony."

Agility is a relatively new sport that came to the United States from England. The handler and the dog, working as a team, go through a timed obstacle course. Scoring is simple and objective, based upon the dog's ability to complete all of the obstacles at the correct speed with which this is accomplished.

In order to compete in this sport, you must belong to an all-breed club or an obedience club where there

The Irish Terrier will stop at no challenge and can be trained to do almost anything. This Irish practices his water retrieval skills.

are individuals who support this event. The obstacle course requires substantial space and the obstacles themselves are fairly extensive.

Many dog shows now hold agility as an exhibition due to its growing popularity. Although your dog must follow commands, this is a sport where both the handler and the dog can have a lot of fun, in addition to getting a lot of exercise. The ring is easy to find because spectators can be four deep around the entire area. A great deal of enthusiasm emanates from all quarters—cheering from the spectators, barking from the dogs, and loud encouragement from the handlers. Agility is a fun sport and not for the weak of heart!

Volunteer work is another rewarding activity that you can do with your Irish Terrier. Bringing your dog to a nursing home once a week will not only bring companionship to an elderly person in need of affection, but will keep your Irish Terrier busy. More importantly, research has determined that volunteer work helps to increase longevity.

Remember, determine early on who is going to be the boss of the household and you will have a wonderful pet who will be a worthy family member and a joy to be around.

Opposite: Gloria Geddes and her two champions take a break and spend a relaxing afternoon at the park.

Research has determined that volunteer work helps to increase longevity and is mentally rewarding. Nancy Petersen and her young pup make a new friend.

SHOWING YOUR IRISH TERRIER

"He is a grand little showman; and when he goes into the ring with his head erect and his flag flying he is as proud of you at one end of the lead as you are of him at the other."

Dog shows have been in existence in America for well over 100 years. The Westminster Kennel Club dog show, held every year in the beginning of February in New York City, is the second oldest annual sporting event in the country, with only the Kentucky Derby having greater longevity.

If you are new to the show ring, attend a few local

Showing your Irish Terrier takes time, patience, and commitment. Ch. Cocksure's Casey The Delaware Diamond and Ch. Cocksure's Mystic Diamond take the honors at the Cudahy Kennel Club.

shows without your dog to see what the game is about. If you are competitive, have the time and the money to compete, and of course, have a good dog, this may be the sport and hobby for you.

Contact your local all-breed club and find out if they offer conformation classes where you can properly learn how to handle your dog in the ring. Start attending these classes on a regular basis. One class does not an expert make! Your all-breed club will hold one or two matches a year and you should plan to attend these. Match shows are run like a dog show, but they are casual and a good place for the beginner to learn. You will not receive any points toward a championship, but you will find out how a dog show is run and learn what will be expected of you and your dog. Entry fees are minimal. This is also a good opportunity to meet the people in the breed.

When you think you are ready—your dog is in coat, can walk on a lead, and you feel confident—enter an AKC-licensed dog show. You should have your Irish Terrier at least in some semblance of a show coat. If you are a novice with a young dog, do not feel embarrassed if your dog doesn't look quite as smart as the one who is with the professional handler. However, while you are in the ring or at ringside, do watch these dogs and handlers and try to learn something from them.

Remember that participating successfully in dog shows requires patience, time, money, skill, and

Ch. Cocksure's Mystic Diamond, or "Amber" to her friends, shows off her exquisite award-winning form. Owned by Robert and Gloria Geddes.

Opposite: Although the Irish Terrier is an energetic and spirited dog, he is also extremely well mannered. Ch. Fighting O'Flynn owned by Stephen Skolnik moves gracefully across the show ring.

talent. It is the only sport where the amateur and the professional compete on an equal footing. The average dog show competitor remains active for only four to five years. Personal commitments such as children, work, and other hobbies can be a problem to those who want to compete every weekend. More often, the competitor who does not win enough will find his interest in the sport waning. A poorly groomed dog, a poorly bred dog, a dog that does not like to show, and a handler who will not take the time to learn how to handle well are all deterrents to staying with the sport of dog showing.

I once showed a rather out-of-coat Scottish Terrier to an old, well-known terrier man and AKC judge (and an Irishman), and after the judging he took me aside and said, "My dear, you don't take your girl to the ball in her dungarees!" And someone wrote the following: "The difference between conditioning a dog for competition in a dog show and the mere dressing him up for acceptance in polite canine society is one of degree rather than of kind, the difference between the primping and grooming and barbering of a man who is about to attend his first wedding and the mere turning oneself out presentably for the daily grind at the office."

For a dog to be show quality, he must be obedient, in good coat, and able to walk on a lead. Ch. Huntermoon Express owned by Bruce and Nancy Petersen.

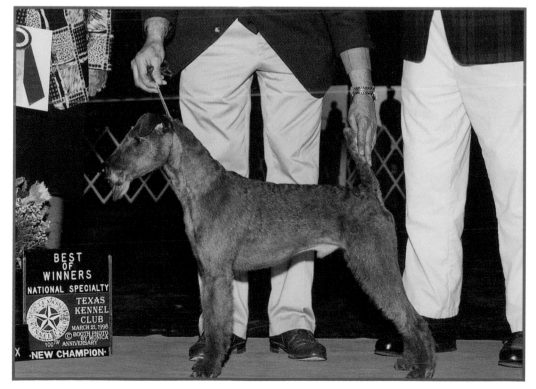

YOUR HEALTHY IRISH TERRIER

By and large, the Irish Terrier is considered to be a healthy breed, relatively free from genetic problems and known for his longevity. Well-bred and well-cared-for animals are less prone to developing diseases and problems than are carelessly bred and neglected animals. Your knowledge of how to avoid problems is far more valuable than all of the books and advice on how to cure them. Respectively, the only person you should listen to about treatment is your vet. Veterinarians don't have all the answers, but at least they are trained to analyze and treat illnesses, and are aware of the full implications of treatments. This does not mean a few old remedies aren't good standbys when all else fails, but in most cases modern science provides the best treatments for disease.

Opposite: As a responsible Irish Terrier owner, you should have a basic understanding of the medical problems that affect the breed.

PHYSICAL EXAMS

Your puppy should receive regular physical examinations or check-ups. These come in two forms. One is obviously performed by your vet, and the other is a day-to-day procedure that should be done by you. Apart from the fact the exam will highlight any problem at an early stage, it is an excellent way of socializing the pup to being handled.

To do the physical exam yourself, start at the head and work your way around the body. You are looking for any sign of lesions, or any indication of parasites on the pup. The most common parasites are fleas and ticks.

78

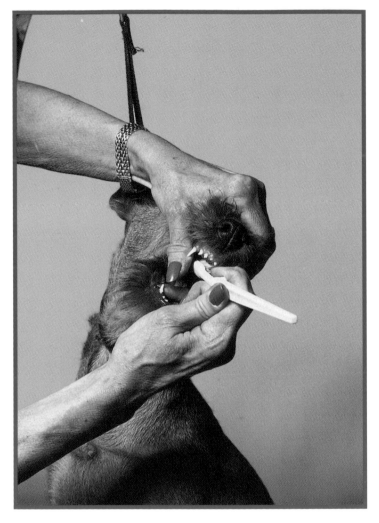

It's important that you take excellent care of your dog's teeth. Brushing will not only keep his teeth strong and healthy, but also help keep his breath fresh.

HEALTHY TEETH AND GUMS

Chewing is instinctual. Puppies chew so that their teeth and jaws grow strong and healthy as they develop. As the permanent teeth begin to emerge, it is painful and annoying to the puppy, and puppy owners must recognize that their new charges need something safe upon which to chew. Unfortunately, once the puppy's permanent teeth have emerged and settled solidly into the jaw, the chewing instinct does not fade. Adult dogs instinctively need to clean their teeth, massage their gums, and exercise their jaws through chewing.

It is necessary for your dog to have clean teeth. You should take your dog to the veterinarian at least once a year to have his teeth cleaned and to have his mouth examined for any sign of oral disease. Although dogs do not get cavities in the same way humans do, dogs'

The Hercules® by Nylabone® has raised dental tips that help fight plaque on your Irish Terrier's teeth and gums.

teeth accumulate tartar, and more quickly than humans do! Veterinarians recommend brushing your dog's teeth daily. But who can find time to brush their dog's teeth daily? The accumulation of tartar and plaque on our dog's teeth when not removed can cause irritation and eventually erode the enamel and finally destroy the teeth. Advanced cases, while destroying the teeth, bring on gingivitis and periodontitis, two very serious conditions that can affect the dog's internal organs as well...to say nothing about bad breath!

Raised dental tips on the surface of every Plaque Attacker™ help to combat plaque and tartar.

Since everyone can't brush their dog's teeth daily or get to the veterinarian often enough for him to scale

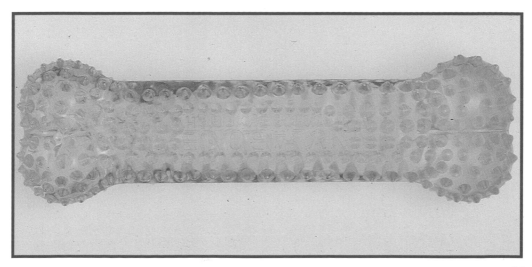

the dog's teeth, providing the dog with something safe to chew on will help maintain oral hygiene. Chew devices from Nylabone® keep dogs' teeth clean, but they also provide an excellent resource for entertainment and relief of doggie tensions. Nylabone® products give your dog something to do for an hour or two every day and during that hour or two, your dog will be taking an active part in keeping his teeth and gums healthy…without even realizing it! That's invaluable to your dog, and valuable to you!

Nylabone® provides fun bones, challenging bones, and *safe* bones. It is an owner's responsibility to recognize safe chew toys from dangerous ones. Your dog will chew and devour anything you give him. Dogs must not be permitted to chew on items that they can break. Pieces of broken objects can do internal damage to a dog, besides ripping the dog's mouth. Cheap plastic or rubber toys can cause stoppage in the intestines; such stoppages are operable only if caught immediately.

The most obvious choices, in this case, may be the worst choice. Natural beef bones were not designed for chewing and cannot take too much pressure from the sides. Due to the abrasive nature of these bones, they should be offered most sparingly. Knuckle bones, though once very popular for dogs, can be easily

Nylabone® is the only plastic dog bone made of 100% virgin nylon, specially processed to create a tough, durable, completely safe bone.

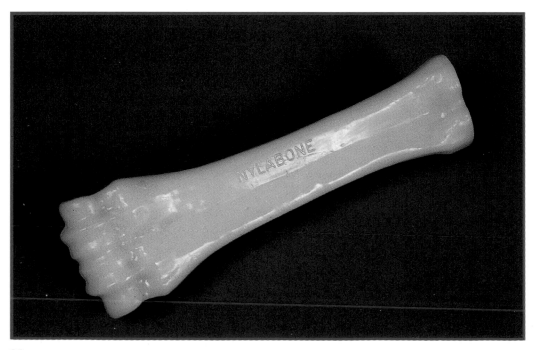

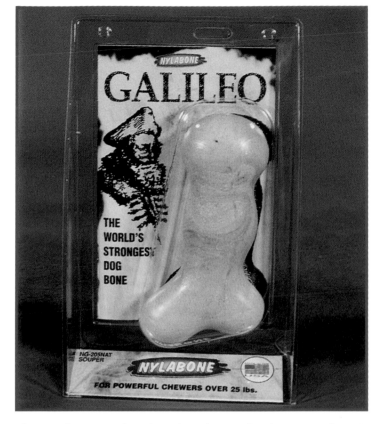

The Galileo™ is flavored to appeal to your dog and annealed so it has a relatively soft outer layer.

chewed up and eaten by dogs. At the very least, digestion is interrupted; at worst, the dog can choke or suffer from intestinal blockage.

When a dog chews hard on a Nylabone®, little bristle-like projections appear on the surface of the bone. These help to clean the dog's teeth and add to the gum-massaging. Given the chemistry of the nylon, the bristle can pass through the dog's intestinal tract without effect. Since nylon is inert, no micro-organism can grow on it, and it can be washed in soap and water or sterilized in boiling water or in an autoclave.

For the sake of your dog, his teeth and your own peace of mind, provide your dog with Nylabones®. They have 100 variations from which to choose.

FIGHTING FLEAS

Fleas are very mobile and may be red, black, or brown in color. The adults suck the blood of the host, while the larvae feed on the feces of the adults, which is rich in blood. Flea "dirt" may be seen on the pup as very tiny clusters of blackish specks that look like freshly ground pepper. The eggs of fleas may be laid on the puppy, though they are more commonly laid off the host in a favorable place, such as the bedding. They normally hatch in 4 to 21 days, depending on the temperature, but they can survive for up to 18 months if temperature conditions are not favorable. The larvae are maggot-like and molt a couple of times before forming pupae, which can survive long periods until the temperature, or the vibration of a nearby host, causes them to emerge and jump on a host.

There are a number of effective treatments available, and you should discuss them with your veterinarian, then follow all instructions for the one you choose. Any treatment will involve a product for your puppy or dog and one for the environment, and will require diligence on your part to treat all areas and thoroughly clean your home and yard until the infestation is eradicated.

THE TROUBLE WITH TICKS

Ticks are arthropods of the spider family, which means they have eight legs (though the larvae have six). They bury their headparts into the host and gorge on its blood. They are easily seen as small grain-like creatures sticking out from the skin. They are often picked up when dogs play in fields, but may also arrive in your yard via wild animals—even birds—or stray cats and dogs. Some ticks are species-specific, others are more adaptable and will host on many species.

The cat flea is the most common flea of dogs. It starts feeding soon after it makes contact with the dog.

The deer tick is the most common carrier of Lyme disease. Photo courtesy of Virbac Laboratories, Inc., Fort Worth, Texas.

The most troublesome type of tick is the deer tick, which spreads the deadly Lyme disease that can cripple a dog (or a person). Deer ticks are tiny and very hard to detect. Often, by the time they're big enough to notice, they've been feeding on the dog for a few days—long enough to do their damage. Lyme disease was named for the area of the United States in which it was first detected—Lyme, Connecticut—but has now been diagnosed in almost all parts of the U.S. Your veterinarian can advise you of the danger to your dog(s) in your area, and may suggest your dog be vaccinated for Lyme. Always go over your dog with a fine-toothed flea comb when you come in from walking through any area that may harbor deer ticks, and if your dog is acting unusually sluggish or sore, seek veterinary advice.

Attempts to pull a tick free will invariably leave the headpart in the pup, where it will die and cause an infected wound or abscess. The best way to remove ticks is to dab a strong saline solution, iodine, or alcohol on them. This will numb them, causing them to loosen their hold, at which time they can be removed with forceps. The wound can then be cleaned and covered with an antiseptic ointment. If ticks are common in your area, consult with your vet for a suitable pesticide to be used in kennels, on bedding, and on the puppy or dog.

INSECTS AND OTHER OUTDOOR DANGERS

There are many biting insects, such as mosquitoes, that can cause discomfort to a puppy. Many diseases are transmitted by the males of these species.

A pup can easily get a grass seed or thorn lodged between his pads or in the folds of his ears. These may go unnoticed until an abscess forms.

This is where your daily check of the puppy or dog will do a world of good. If your puppy has been playing in long grass or places where there may be thorns, pine needles, wild animals, or parasites, the check-up is a wise precaution.

There are many dangers in the great outdoors that your dog can encounter, so closely supervise him when he is outside.

SKIN DISORDERS

Apart from problems associated with lesions created by biting pests, a puppy may fall foul to a number of other skin disorders. Examples are ringworm, mange, and eczema. Ringworm is not caused by a worm, but is a fungal infection. It manifests itself as a sore-looking bald circle. If your puppy should have any form of bald patches, let your veterinarian check him over; a microscopic examination can confirm the condition. Many old remedies for ringworm exist, such as iodine, carbolic acid, formalin, and other tinctures, but modern drugs are superior.

Fungal infections can be very difficult to treat, and even more difficult to eradicate, because of the spores. These can withstand most treatments, other than burning, which is the best thing to do with bedding once the condition has been confirmed.

Mange is a general term that can be applied to many skin conditions where the hair falls out and a flaky crust develops and falls away.

Often, dogs will scratch themselves, and this invariably is worse than the original condition, for it opens lesions that are then subject to viral, fungal, or parasitic attack. The cause of the problem can be various species of mites. These either live on skin debris and the hair follicles, which they destroy, or they bury themselves just beneath the skin and feed on the tissue. Applying general remedies from pet stores is not recommended because it is essential to identify the type of mange before a specific treatment is effective.

Eczema is another non-specific term applied to many skin disorders. The condition can be brought about in many ways. Sunburn, chemicals, allergies to foods, drugs, pollens, and even stress can all produce a deterioration of the skin and coat. Given the range of causal factors, treatment can be difficult because the problem is one of identification. It is a case of taking each possibility at a time and trying to correctly diagnose the matter. If the cause is of a dietary nature then you must remove one item at a time in order to find out if the dog is allergic to a given food. It could, of course, be the lack of a nutrient that is the problem, so if the condition persists, you should consult your veterinarian.

INTERNAL DISORDERS

It cannot be overstressed that it is very foolish to attempt to diagnose an internal disorder without the advice of a veterinarian. Take a relatively common problem such as diarrhea. It might be caused by nothing more serious than the puppy hogging a lot of food or eating something that it has never previously eaten. Conversely, it could be the first indication of a potentially fatal disease. It's up to your veterinarian to make the correct diagnosis.

The following symptoms, especially if they accompany each other or are progressively added to earlier symptoms, mean you should visit the veterinarian right away:

Continual vomiting. All dogs vomit from time to time and this is not necessarily a sign of illness. They will eat grass to induce vomiting. It is a natural cleansing process common to many carnivores. However, continued vomiting is a clear sign of a problem. It may be a blockage in the pup's intestinal tract, it may be induced by worms, or it could be due to any number of diseases.

Diarrhea. This, too, may be nothing more than a temporary condition due to many factors. Even a change of home can induce diarrhea, because this often stresses the pup, and invariably there is some change in the diet. If it persists more than 48 hours then something is amiss. If blood is seen in the feces, waste no time at all in taking the dog to the vet.

Running eyes and/or nose. A pup might have a chill and this will cause the eyes and nose to weep. Again, this should quickly clear up if the puppy is placed in a warm environment and away from any drafts. If it does not, and especially if a mucous discharge is seen, then the pup has an illness that must be diagnosed.

Coughing. Prolonged coughing is a sign of a problem, usually of a respiratory nature.

Wheezing. If the pup has difficulty breathing and makes a wheezing sound when breathing, then something is wrong.

Cries when attempting to defecate or urinate. This might only be a minor problem due to the hard state of the feces, but it could be more serious, especially if the pup cries when urinating.

Cries when touched. Obviously, if you do not handle a puppy with care he might yelp. However, if he cries even when lifted gently, then he has an internal problem that becomes apparent when pressure is applied to a given area of the body. Clearly, this must be diagnosed.

Refuses food. Generally, puppies and dogs are greedy creatures when it comes to feeding time. Some might be more fussy, but none should refuse more than one meal. If they go for a number of hours without showing any interest in their food, then something is not as it should be.

General listlessness. All puppies have their off days when they do not seem their usual cheeky, mischievous selves. If this condition persists for more than two days then there is little doubt of a problem. They may not show any of the signs listed, other than perhaps a reduced interest in their food. There are many diseases that can develop internally without displaying obvious clinical signs. Blood, fecal, and other tests are needed in order to identify the disorder before it reaches an advanced state that may not be treatable.

WORMS

There are many species of worms, and a number of these live in the tissues of dogs and most other animals. Many create no problem at all, so you are not even aware they exist. Others can be tolerated in small levels, but become a major problem if they number more than a few. The most common types seen in dogs are roundworms and tapeworms. While roundworms are the greater problem, tapeworms require an intermediate host so are more easily eradicated.

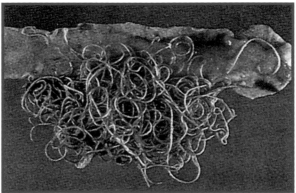

Roundworms are spaghetti-like worms that cause a pot-bellied appearance and dull coat, along with more severe symptoms, such as diarrhea and vomiting. Photo courtesy of Merck AgVet.

Roundworms of the species *Toxocara canis* infest the dog. They may grow to a length of 8 inches (20 cm) and look like strings of spaghetti. The worms feed on the digesting food in the pup's intestines. In chronic cases the puppy will become pot-bellied, have diarrhea, and will vomit. Eventually, he will stop eating, having passed through the stage when he always seems hungry. The worms lay eggs in the puppy and these pass out in his feces. They are then either ingested by the pup, or they are eaten by mice, rats, or beetles. These may then be eaten by the puppy and the life cycle is complete.

Larval worms can migrate to the womb of a pregnant bitch, or to her mammary glands, and this is how they pass to the puppy. The pregnant bitch can be wormed, which will help. The pups can, and should,

Whipworms are hard to find unless you strain your dog's feces, and this is best left to a veterinarian. Pictured here are adult whipworms.

be wormed when they are about two weeks old. Repeat worming every 10 to 14 days and the parasites should be removed. Worms can be extremely dangerous to young puppies, so you should be sure the pup is wormed as a matter of routine.

Tapeworms can be seen as tiny rice-like eggs sticking to the puppy's or dog's anus. They are less destructive, but still undesirable. The eggs are eaten by mice, fleas, rabbits, and other animals that serve as intermediate hosts. They develop into a larval stage and the host must be eaten by the dog in order to complete the chain. Your vet will supply a suitable remedy if tapeworms are seen or suspected. There are other worms, such as hookworms and whipworms, that are also blood suckers. They will make a pup anemic, and blood might be seen in the feces, which can be examined by the vet to confirm their presence. Cleanliness in all matters is the best preventative measure for all worms.

Heartworm infestation in dogs is passed by mosquitoes but can be prevented by a monthly (or daily) treatment that is given orally. Talk to your vet about the risk of heartworm in your area.

BLOAT (GASTRIC DILATATION)

This condition has proved fatal in many dogs, especially large and deep-chested breeds, such as the Weimaraner and the Great Dane. However, any dog can get bloat. It is caused by swallowing air during exercise, food/water gulping or another strenuous task. As many believe, it is not the result of flatulence. The stomach of an affected dog twists, disallowing food and blood flow and resulting in harmful toxins being released into the bloodstream. Death can easily follow if the condition goes undetected.

The best preventative measure is not to feed large meals or exercise your puppy or dog immediately after he has eaten. Veterinarians recommend feeding three smaller meals per day in an elevated feeding rack, adding water to dry food to prevent gulping, and not offering water during mealtimes.

VACCINATIONS

Every puppy, purebred or mixed breed, should be vaccinated against the major canine diseases. These are distemper, leptospirosis, hepatitis, and canine parvovirus. Your puppy may have received a temporary vaccination against distemper before you purchased him, but be sure to ask the breeder to be sure.

The age at which vaccinations are given can vary, but will usually be when the pup is 8 to 12 weeks old. By this time any protection given to the pup by antibodies received from his mother via her initial milk feeds will be losing their strength.

Rely on your veterinarian for the most effectual vaccination schedule for your Irish Terrier puppy.

The puppy's immune system works on the basis that the white blood cells engulf and render harmless

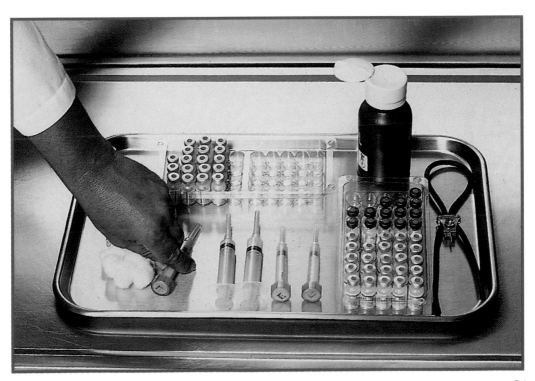

attacking bacteria. However, they must first recognize a potential enemy.

Vaccines are either dead bacteria or they are live, but in very small doses. Either type prompts the pup's defense system to attack them. When a large attack then comes (if it does), the immune system recognizes it and massive numbers of lymphocytes (white blood corpuscles) are mobilized to counter the attack. However, the ability of the cells to recognize these dangerous viruses can diminish over a period of time. It is therefore useful to provide annual reminders about the nature of the enemy. This is done by means of booster injections that keep the immune system on its alert. Immunization is not 100-percent guaranteed to be successful, but is very close. Certainly it is better than giving the puppy no protection.

Dogs are subject to other viral attacks, and if these are of a high-risk factor in your area, then your vet will suggest you have the puppy vaccinated against these as well.

Your puppy or dog should also be vaccinated against the deadly rabies virus. In fact, in many places it is illegal for your dog not to be vaccinated. This is to protect your dog, your family, and the rest of the animal population from this deadly virus that infects the nervous system and causes dementia and death.

ACCIDENTS

All puppies will get their share of bumps and bruises due to the rather energetic way they play. These will usually heal themselves over a few days. Small cuts should be bathed with a suitable disinfectant and then smeared with an antiseptic ointment. If a cut looks more serious, then stem the flow of blood with a towel or makeshift tourniquet and rush the pup to the veterinarian. Never apply so much pressure to the wound that it might restrict the flow of blood to the limb.

In the case of burns you should apply cold water or an ice pack to the surface. If the burn was due to a chemical, then this must be washed away with copious amounts of water. Apply petroleum jelly, or any vegetable oil, to the burn. Trim away the hair if need be. Wrap the dog in a blanket and rush him to the vet. The pup may go into shock, depending on the severity of the burn, and this will result in a lowered blood pressure, which is dangerous and the reason the pup must receive immediate veterinary attention.

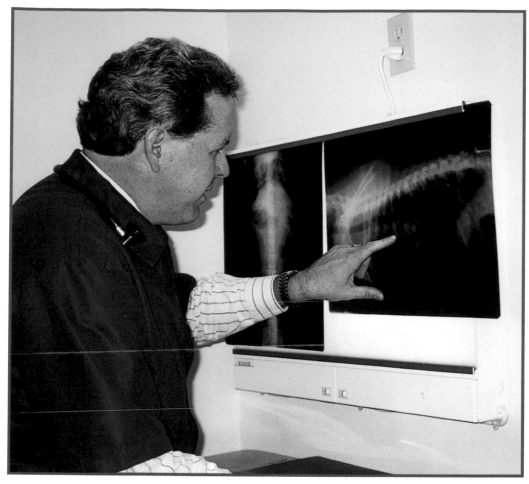

It is a good idea to x-ray the chest and abdomen on any dog hit by a car.

If a broken limb is suspected then try to keep the animal as still as possible. Wrap your pup or dog in a blanket to restrict movement and get him to the veterinarian as soon as possible. Do not move the dog's head so it is tilting backward, as this might result in blood entering the lungs.

Do not let your pup jump up and down from heights, as this can cause considerable shock to the joints. Like all youngsters, puppies do not know when enough is enough, so you must do all their thinking for them.

Provided you apply strict hygiene to all aspects of raising your puppy, and you make daily checks on his physical state, you have done as much as you can to safeguard him during his most vulnerable period. Routine visits to your veterinarian are also recommended, especially while the puppy is under one year of age. The vet may notice something that did not seem important to you.

HEAD
Long, but in proportion

EARS
V-shaped, dropping forward

EYES
Dark brown, intense

NOSE
Black

TEETH
Strong, even, neith
undershot nor ove